The Great Concern

The Great Concern

Preparation for Death

Edward Pearse

REFORMATION HERITAGE BOOKS
Grand Rapids, Michigan

The Great Concern
© 2020 by Soli Deo Gloria

Soli Deo Gloria Publications
An imprint of Reformation Heritage Books
2965 Leonard St., NE
Grand Rapids, MI 49525
616-977-0889
orders@heritagebooks.org
www.heritagebooks.org

Printed in the United States of America
20 21 22 23 24 25/10 9 8 7 6 5 4 3 2 1

Library of Congress Cataloging-in-Publication Data

Names: Pearse, Edward, 1633?-1674?, author.
Title: The great concern : preparation for death / Edward Pearse.
Description: Grand Rapids, Michigan : Soli Deo Gloria Publications, 2020.
Identifiers: LCCN 2020024187 (print) | LCCN 2020024188 (ebook) | ISBN 9781601787941 (hardcover) | ISBN 9781601787958 (epub)
Subjects: LCSH: Death—Religious aspects—Christianity. | Future life—Christianity.
Classification: LCC BT825 .P38 2020 (print) | LCC BT825 (ebook) | DDC 236/.1–dc23
LC record available at https://lccn.loc.gov/2020024187
LC ebook record available at https://lccn.loc.gov/2020024188

For additional Reformed literature, request a free book list from Reformation Heritage Books at the above address.

CONTENTS

TO THE READER

If you are one who indeed lives in the belief of a future life, an eternity of happiness or misery, when time and day shall be no more, I am confident the ensuing discourse will be grateful and welcome to you. I make no apology for its plainness, nor am I at all solicitous touching the censures I may fall under for publishing it. If you will read it with an upright heart, I question not but through a blessing from above it may do your soul good. Sure I am, you will find the argument most weighty and the concern thereof most important. And woe be to that soul which misses the design it tends to and aims at.

When men come to die, and to find themselves launching forth into the vast ocean of eternity, at least when once they find themselves encircled in that ocean (which quickly they do, when once death makes its approach), then they see that their great interest lay beyond this poor, vain, perishing world and the things thereof; then they see that their great concern was to have looked and lived beyond time and days, and have made provision for an eternal state; but alas! alas! then it is too late. Then they cry out, O eternity, eternity! O miserable souls that we are! How did sin and the world blind and bewitch us, that we could not ere now, when it is too late, see the weight of an eternal interest! O blind and brutish creatures that are merely taken with carnal and sensual things pleasing only to a sensual appetite, and forgot God, the chief good, the things of heaven and a blessed eternity, which would have made us happy forever.

Now to prevent these doubtful lamentations, and such a dismal and remediless shipwreck of eternal souls, as also to show them the path of life and to engage them to make sure of a blessed eternity, while time and days last, is the design of the ensuing discourse and of the dying author in it. And the Lord, the God of all grace, prosper it in order thereunto. God has kept me for a full half year by the grave side. One while lifting me up, then casting me down, and now He seems to be speedily finishing my days. To whom, through the infinite riches of free grace, I can with some comfort and boldness say, "Come, Lord Jesus, come quickly, Amen." And now, farewell, vain world; farewell, friends and relations; farewell, eating and drinking; and, blessed be God, farewell, sin and sinning. Within a few days I shall sin no more, nor ever be in a possibility of sinning, but shall be like my Lord, and shall see Him as He is. And lastly, farewell, reader.

—E. P.

$\mathcal{A}$re You $\mathcal{P}$repared to $\mathcal{D}$ie?

*Which contains an introduction and an explication of the
words of the text, with the general truth of them, and thereto
the foundation of our intended discourse.*

> *O spare me, that I may recover strength,
> before I go hence, and be no more.*
> —PSALM 39:13

To walk with God here on earth while we live, and to be ready
to live with God forever in heaven when we come to die, is
the great work we have to do, the great concern we have to
mind, in our present pilgrimage. To grow great and high in
the world, to build our names and families, to live a life of
sensual pleasures and delights, spending our days in mirth—
these are low and mean poor things, things infinitely beneath
the dignity of a soul and altogether unworthy of the least of
its care and solicitude. But to know God, to obey God, to love
God, to delight in God, to contemplate the glorious excellencies and perfections of God, to live upon God, and to live
to God—upon Him as our chief good and happiness, and to
Him as our life's end, and withal to be found ready at last to
live with Him forever, to enter upon the beatifical vision, and
to pass into the life of love and holiness, which the saints and

angels live above, being made perfect in the vision and fruition of the God of glory—this is truly noble; this is worthy of
the care and solicitude of souls. To promote those things, and
especially the latter, is my design in fixing my meditations on
this Scripture, which I am the rather induced to do because I
am apprehensive that the time of my going hence, when I shall
be seen no more, is drawing very nigh. The words are a holy
and prophetical wish and desire breathed out into the bosom
of God by the man after His own heart, and that when under
sore and heavy afflictions; under sickness, say some; under
great straits and distresses, by reason of Absalom's rebellion
and conspiracy against him, say others. In this wish or desire
of his, you may note three things.

(1) What that is which he wishes for or desires of God,
and that is, sparing mercy. "O spare me."

(2) The end of this wish or desire of his, and that is the
recovery of strength. "O spare me, that I may recover
strength."

(3) The ground or motive which induced him to make
this desire for this end, and that was the near approach
of his death in these words, "Before I go hence,
and be no more" seen. I will briefly paraphrase the
words for the opening of them and then give you the
sum of them, as also my intention for them, in one
general proposition.

"O spare me," that is, cease to smite and afflict me, give
me the relaxation, a breathing time, so one expounds. "Deal
gently and mildly with me," says another. "Withdraw Thy hand
a little from scourging me and mitigate the violence of my
afflictions," say others. "That I may recover strength, that I may
recruit myself a little," says one. "That I may have a breathing
time before my death and, being well composed, may lay down
my Spirit and commit it into Thy hand," say others. "That I
may grow strong in grace and holiness," say others. "That I may

finish my course, and fight a good fight, obtaining the victory through a happy death," say others. The sum is that I may set things right in my soul and get into a more ready posture for my death and dissolution, which seems to be near at hand.

"Before I go hence and be no more"—that is, before I die, never more to return into this life, before I quit this world and bid adieu to this mortal life, to be no more in the land of the living, to be no more in this world, to do anything for God or my soul. For (as one well observes) David does not here suppose death to be the utter end, or annihilation of man, the putting of a man out of being. But his meaning is that if God did still go on to afflict him as He had done, he must suddenly die, suddenly go off the stage of this world, and go down to the bars of death, to the gates of the grave, where as to anything that is to be done for God, or a man's soul, it is as if he were out of being, and where he will be kept forever from returning any more to this life or any opportunity of ever doing anything for another world.

It is a phrase like to and of the same importance with that of Job 16:22, where Job speaks of himself, "When a few years are come, then I shall go the way whence I shall not return." "Not return," that is, not any more to this life, not returning to do anything for God or my soul. The sum of the whole seems to be thus: the good man's afflictions were so pressing and heavy upon him that they did ever bow him down to the grave, and he really looked upon himself as a dying man, as one going down to the dust of the earth where he knew full well nothing was to be done for another life, and from whence there was no return to this life to be expected anymore. Therefore, he requests a breathing time, a little space wherein to recover himself out of all present distempers and discomposure of heart and to set all things right in the matter of his soul, thereby fitting and preparing himself the better for his departure out of this world; he begs a time of respite wherein to prepare himself and make ready for a dying hour. This is the sum of what he drives at and pleads with God for, according to the observation, and therein the sum of my intention shall be this:

> That it is a very desirable thing, and a business of the highest moment and importance to the children of men, to have all things set right, well ordered, and composed, in the matters of their souls before they leave this world, to get all the spiritual concerns of their souls into the best posture they can before a dying hour comes.

David, a holy man, a man in covenant with God—yea, a man after God's own heart—does yet (you see) pray for sparing mercy, for a breathing time, a time of respite here in this world before he goes off the stage. And why so? That he might recover strength, that he might set things right in the matters of his soul, that he might make himself more ready and get his spiritual concerns into a better posture for a dying hour; and this he looked at, and made out after, as that which was most desirable and of the highest importance to him, as indeed it is to all. You have a Scripture not unlike to this: "Are not my days few? cease then, and let me alone, that I may take comfort a little, before I go whence I shall not return, even to the land of darkness and the shadow of death" (Job 10:20–21). That I may take comfort a little, that I may recover a little, that I may have a breathing time, that I may recover myself and gather up my spirits. So I find the phrase expounded. He seems to desire a breathing time, the better to compose himself, and the matters of his soul, for a dying hour. And indeed it is the concern of us all, to set all things right in our souls and to get into the readiest posture that possibly we can, for when a dying hour comes. I shall first briefly evince this truth and then make some practical improvement of it. SHOW CLEARLY

CHAPTER 2

An Important and Hard Task

Wherein is shown the exceeding great weight of dying work, and the extreme difficulty of a dying hour, as the first evidence of our assertion.

Dying work, my beloved, is great work, and a dying hour is a difficult hour; therefore, we had need to have all things well-ordered and ready in the matters of our souls against that time, that work, when that hour comes. I will lay the weight of dying work and the difficulty of a dying hour before you in four propositions.

The first proposition is this: that death (in itself and in its own nature, if we look no further) is a very terrible thing; and we had need have all things set right in our souls, all things in order when we encounter it. The philosopher Aristotle, who looked not beyond the natural notion of death, called it the most terrible of all terrible things. And in Job 18:14 the Holy Ghost Himself calls it "the king of terrors." His "confidence," speaking of a wicked man, "shall bring him to the king of terrors"—that is, to death, which is most formidable. Indeed, it is therefore called the king of terrors because it is the greatest and strongest terror. And death must needs be terrible in itself:

(1) Because it deprives us of all our sweet comforts and enjoyments here in this world and puts an eternal period to our fruition of them. Here we enjoy much good, many dreams which run pleasantly on each hand of us (it may be); but when death comes, that deprives us of all. "Naked came I out of my mother's womb, and naked shall I return thither" (Job 1:21). So the apostle, "For we brought nothing into this world, and it is certain we can carry nothing out," speaking as to our outward comforts here (1 Tim. 6:7). The psalmist to the same effect speaks of a rich man: "He shall carry nothing away: his glory," says he, "shall not descend after him" (Ps. 49:17). Death, as one observes, the greatest leveler in the world, levels scepters and plowshares; it makes the prince poor as the peasant.

(2) Because it dissolves the union between the soul and the body. Death is indeed the rending of body and soul (those old and loving companions) asunder. Now all disunions (as a worthy divine observes) are uncomfortable, and some disunions are terrible. And, as some disunions are terrible, so those are of all others most terrible that do rend them from us. Now what union is so near as that between the soul and body? And therefore what disunion is so terrible as the dissolution of this union? The dissolving of the union between a man and his wife is terrible because they are nearly united to each other, but the dissolving of the union between soul and body is more terrible because the union is more near and close. A man and his wife "are one flesh," but the soul and body make but one person. Now death dissolves this union. While we live, the soul dwells in the body, informs the body, acts in and by the body; it has a great influence upon, and is greatly influenced by, the body. But when death comes, then the soul and body part till the resurrection, one returning "to the earth as it was: and the spirit shall return unto God who gave it" (Eccl. 12:7).

(3) It is a destroying and demolishing of the body of man, that famous and curious fabric, and a bringing it into dust and putrefaction (Ps. 90:3). It turns a living body into a dead carcass, a lifeless lump of clay, and causes it to become meat for worms to feed on (Job 19:26). The body of man is a very curious piece of workmanship, such as wherein the infinite power and wisdom of God is much seen and manifested (Ps. 139:14–15). But when death comes, it mars and demolishes all, stains all its beauty, and draws a veil upon all its glory. Sickness often makes a man's beauty to "consume away like a moth," as you have it in Psalm 39:11. But death utterly defaces it, and draws a veil upon it. That turns his beauty into blackness and deformity. One of the ancients, standing by Caesar's tomb, wept, saying, "Where is now the beauty of Caesar? What now is become of all his magnificence?" In a word, as life is the sweetest of all outward mercies, so death is the sharpest of all outward afflictions. The pains of it are pains to a proverb. The sorrows of it are sorrows to a proverb. "The sorrows of death compassed me" (Ps. 116:3). Now if death be to us terrible in itself, then judge you whether we had not need to have all things ready and in order when it comes.

(2) The second proposition is that in a dying hour, the devil is most fierce and terrible in his assaults and temptations upon the soul. The devil is in Scripture called a "roaring lion" and is usually most so against the poor people of God when they come to die. Then he had wrath, because he knows his time is short, to allude to Revelation 12:12. When a man or woman comes to die, the devil knows he has but a short time to tempt, to vex, to terrify that soul in, and therefore then usually he exercises great wrath; then he stirs up all his wrath, all his malice, all his cruelty against him; he sees this is the last cast he is like to have for it, the last onset he is like to make upon the soul's faith and comfort, and that now the battle is won or left

forever. Therefore, now he roars and rages terribly indeed, now he discharges all his murdering pieces against the soul, to make batteries, if possible, upon the soul's fort of salvation and to shake its foundation of life and happiness.

The devil is the enemy of souls (Matt. 13:25), and his enmity works especially one of these two ways: either, first, to keep them from life and happiness, and here he acts rather like an angel of light rather than a roaring lion. He works rather in a way of flattery than in a way of terror. Hence we read of his wiles, methods, devices, and the like—his cunning and fallacious workings thereby to destroy souls. Or, secondly, to trouble and torment souls in their way to life and happiness, and here he is indeed like a roaring lion, and never more than when we come to die.

There are among others two seasons wherein the devil is most fierce and terrible in his assaults upon the soul. The first is when a man is going from sin to grace, when he is fully resolved to close with Christ, to shake off the yoke of sin, and to take upon him the yoke of Jesus. The second is when a man is going from grace to glory—when a man begins to live that spiritual life and when a man comes to die the natural death. I know, first, that as for his own children, Satan usually lets them alone when they come to die. He is afraid to have them disturbed, though sometimes he cannot forbear but torment them before their time.

Second, God can and sometimes does chain him up so that he shall not be able to trouble and torment the saints in their passage out of this world. Yet still, I say, for the most part he does fiercely assault them then; and doubtless there are but very few of the children of God but do meet with very sore assaults from Satan when they come to die. Then he turns accuser; then he charges the soul with all its sins; then he tells him he is a hypocrite, that all his profession has been nothing but a delusion and the like. Now is Satan thus fierce and terrible in his assaults upon the soul in a dying hour! Surely, then, we need to have all things ready for when that hour comes.

③ The third proposition is this: that in a dying hour conscience is most awakened and so most alive and smart in its threats and charges against the soul if all be not right within, and therefore we need to have all so in that hour. There are three seasons in which conscience is most awake in the soul. First, when God begins to deal with the soul in order to life and salvation. Then God lets conscience loose upon a man. Hence we read of them that they "were pricked at their heart" in the sense of sin. The word is, they were pricked through and through (Acts 2:37). And, says Paul, "Sin revived, and I died" (Rom. 7:9). That is, in the sight of my sin, which was wrought in me by the law of God, I was made to see myself lost and miserable, and awakened out of my security. Second, when the soul is under some smart and notable affliction from the hand of God. This is evident in that instance of Joseph's brethren, whose consciences were awakened when they were in distress and charged them with the guilt of their sin in selling their brother (Gen. 42:21). Third, when a man comes to die, when the visions of death and the grave are before him. Oh! You little think how strict conscience will be in its search, how sharp in its charge, and how severe in its censure in a dying hour. Then if there be but the least frown in God's face toward the soul, the least flaw in his peace, the least blot or blur in his evidences for heaven—if there be but the least stain upon the spirit, the least sin unpardoned, unrepented of—it is a thousand to one but conscience will take notice of it and charge the soul with it.

You will find a great deal of difference between conscience upon a bed of ease and conscience upon a sickbed, between conscience in an hour of health and worldly prosperity and conscience in a dying hour. In the one, great things bear but little weight; but in the other, little things usually bear great weight in conscience. Then the language of conscience to the soul is, "These and these things have you done; thus and thus things stand with you. At best, grace is thus and thus weak, corruption thus and thus strong, temptation thus and thus prevalent, the heart thus and thus out of frame, the spirit thus and thus alienated from God," and the like. Hence it is that at death there are such confessions as you have sometimes from men and women, that now they will send for some godly minister or Christian to pray with them and for them, though perhaps they could not endure prayer all their lifetime before. Now if in a dying hour conscience be thus quick and smart in its threats and charges against the soul, then surely we had need, and it is greatly our concern, to have all ready and in order against that hour.

The fourth proposition is this: that in a dying hour we shall have to do with God in a very stupendous and amazing way, in such a way as may well startle and affright us to think of it. We are said to "have to do" with God here (Heb. 4:13). We have here to do with God in duties, in ordinances, in mercies, in afflictions. Indeed, we had as good never have to do with these unless we have to do with God in these. But though we have to do with God here while we live, yet know we shall have to do with God in another sort of way when we come to die, in such a way as may overwhelm us to think of it. I shall give it to you in three steps. Then we have to do with God immediately, with God immediately as our Judge, with God immediately as our Judge for eternity. And how loud do these things call upon us to get all in order in the matters of our souls against a dying hour comes.

(1) When a man comes to die, he has to do with God immediately, and that is an astonishing thing. In death the body crumbles to dust, but "the spirit shall return unto God who gave it." So the Holy Ghost tells us (Eccl. 12:7). The body which came from the dust crumbles to dust again. But the soul goes into God's immediate presence, to deal and to treat with Him, as it were, face-to-face. The soul is always with God and cannot possibly be out of His presence (Ps. 139:7). And yet here the Holy Ghost tells us that when we die, the soul returns to God, intimating that then the soul goes into the immediate presence of God and has more immediately to do with Him than here he was ever prone to have; then he beholds His naked majesty and glory. Now what an astonishing thing is this. You will find (if you observe) that the saints of God—yea, the holiest of them— when they have dealt with God in a more immediate way than ordinary, they have been overwhelmed by it. Take for instance Daniel, who upon receiving visions from God tells us, "There remained no strength in me: for my comeliness was turned in me into corruption" (Dan. 10:8). I might instance also in John, who upon a view of and converse with Christ that was a little more immediate than ordinary "fell at his feet as dead" (Rev. 1:17). Also, that of Jacob: "I have seen God face to face, and my life is preserved," says he, intimating it as a wonder that he could so immediately see God and live (Gen. 32:30). Now if we are to deal with God immediately when we come to die, we had need have all in order before a dying hour comes.

(2) When a man comes to die, he has to do with God immediately, as his Judge: as one that is to try him for his life, to pass sentence upon his soul, to determine his state in righteousness, measuring out life or death, happiness or vengeance to Him in the other world. And is not this an astonishing and an amazing thing? "Then," says Solomon, speaking of death, "shall the dust return to the earth as it was: and the spirit shall

return unto God who gave it" (Eccl. 12:7). At death the spirit returns to God, but it is to God, as a Judge, to determine his future condition for him. "We must all stand before the judgment seat of Christ" and every one must give an account of himself to God. So the Scripture tells us (2 Cor. 5:10). And "It is appointed unto men once to die, but after this the judgment" (Heb. 9:27). When a man comes to die, that which is immediately before him is the judgment of God—the strict, the righteous, the impartial judgment of God—and then away goes the soul into the immediate presence of God, as sitting on a throne of judgment, to pass a sentence of life or death, salvation or damnation, upon him. And (believe it) we had need to have all things set right, and well-ordered in our souls when we come thus to deal with Him. We had need have all things well-ordered and set right in matters of our souls when we deal with God but as sitting upon a throne of grace, but much more when we come to deal with Him as sitting upon a throne of judgment, to conclude and determine our future condition, what it shall be. Judgment is an astonishing and terrifying thing. The hearing of it made Felix "tremble," or (as the word is) it turned him into terror or affrightment (Acts 24:25). And the apostle calls it the "terror of the Lord" (2 Cor. 5:11). Now when a man comes to die, then he says, or may say, "Now I am to deal with the great God, the Judge of all. Now I must appear before His righteous tribunal and have the state of my soul determined for life or death, salvation or damnation in the other world." O how great a thing is this!

(3) When a man comes to die, he has to do with God immediately, as his Judge for eternity. And this speaks it more terrifying and astonishing. For though a man is then to deal with God immediately, and that as his Judge too, yet if it were but for a time for some short term of years, it would not be altogether such a terrifying and amazing thing. But alas! It

is for eternity, and therefore His judgment is called "eternal judgment" (Heb. 6:2). Hence Augustine, speaking of death, called it the gate of eternity—that is, the gate or door that lets men out into eternity: an eternity of life or death, salvation or damnation, the sentence which God will then pass upon the soul will be an eternal sentence, and the soul must be eternally under the execution of it, whether it be for life or death, salvation or damnation. When a man comes to die, he then sees himself launching forth into the great ocean of eternity; he sees his eternal all to be immediately at stake and his eternal state to be immediately determined by the great and holy God. Now he sees he must shoot the great gulf and take up his abode in the eternal region.

This fills him with amazement. "O now," says he, "a sentence must pass upon me once for all. Now I must shoot the great gulf; now I must launch forth into the great ocean, where neither bounds nor bottom is to be found forever. Now I must enter upon eternal joys or eternal flames and endless life either with God or devils, in heaven or hell. Now I shall find infiniteness and eternity combine to do their utmost, to make me happy or miserable forever. Now I must become the immediate object either of infinite wrath or infinite love, infinite hatred or infinite delight, and that forever. And O what an astonishing thing is this! O eternity, eternity! O vast eternity! O great eternity! O boundless eternity!" One serious view of it is enough to amaze a poor soul looking upon it at a distance.

But how much more amazing must it needs be when it shall be before the soul and he sees he must enter upon it the next hour? O then it will be amazing indeed! Astonishing indeed! This one thing, eternity, puts infinite sweetness into mercies and infinite bitterness into sufferings. The thought of this was that which did so much amaze that good man, who sitting in a deep muse a long time, and being asked the reason for it, was silent; and being asked again and again, at length broke out into these words, "For ever, for ever, for ever, for ever," and for near a quarter of an hour together spoke nothing else, thereby telling them that asked him that it was the thoughts of this same forever that so much overwhelmed him. And if you were more in the thoughts of the weight of eternity, you would see it were an astonishing thing indeed. And this is that which makes dying work such a weighty work and a dying hour such a difficult hour.

I will close this head, and with that, this demonstration, with a saying I have read in one of the ancients: "That is not to be accounted," says he, "an evil death, which has had a good life preceding it; nor does anything make death terrible, but that which follows death. Therefore they which must necessarily die are not much to concern themselves, what falls out to cause death but whither by death they are constrained to go, whither death carries them." It is a great saying, and indeed it is no great matter when we die or how we die or what is the occasion of our death. But it is whither death carries us and where death sets us down: whether in a blessed or wretched eternity, whether with God or devils, in heaven or hell. Well, then, if death be thus terrible in its own nature, if in a dying hour the devil be so fierce and terrible in his assault upon souls, if conscience be awakened and smart in its charges and accusations, if then we must have to do with God immediately, and as our Judge—yea, as our Judge for eternity, as One that will determine the eternal conditions of our souls, in unspeakable happiness or unspeakable misery—then surely dying work is great work, and a dying hour is a difficult hour. It then greatly concerns us to have all ready, and all in order in the matters of our souls when the time thereof comes.

CHAPTER 3

Attaining Victory and Glory

Which showeth the glory, sweetness, and blessedness of the attainment of having all things set right in the matters of our souls before a dying hour comes, which will further evince the truth asserted.

As dying work is weighty work, and a dying hour is a difficult hour, so to have all things set right, all well-ordered and composed in the matters of our souls against such an hour comes, is a high, a sweet, and a blessed attainment, an attainment which carries infinite sweetness and suitableness in it, a taste of which I shall give you in two things only. First, hereby we come to be glorious conquerors over death and the grave. Second, hereby we are to have abundant entrance ministered to us into heaven and glory. And, my beloved, what is more sweet and desirable than this? Surely this speaks it to be a very sweet and blessed attainment.

First, hereby we come to be glorious conquerors over death and the grave. Death is an enemy; it is the last enemy the children of God have to grapple and conflict with: "The last enemy that shall be destroyed is death" (1 Cor. 15:26). And being the last enemy in conquering this, they conquer all; conquering this, they are complete and eternal conquerors.

Now, by having all things set right in the matters of our souls, all things ready, and in order for a dying hour, we come to conquer this last enemy—yea, to get a glorious conquest over it. Hereby death comes to be "swallowed up in victory," as you have the expression (1 Cor. 15:54). Hereby "we are more than conquerors" over it (Rom. 8:37). Take the conquest which this gives us over death, in these three things.

(1) Hereby the soul is carried above the fear of death; in Hebrews 2:15 we read of some "who through fear of death were all their lifetime subject to bondage." And if in their lifetime, much more when they come to a dying hour; then conscience (as you heard) is more awake. O the fears, the terrors, the hell upon earth that the sight of death's approach fills many a poor soul withal! But now take a soul that has all things right, and in order in his spiritual concerns, and he is carried above the fear of this king of terrors, and that when made as terrible as the wit and malice of man can possibly make it. He can converse with his last enemy as one who has lost its sting and power, and so without the least fear or dismay of spirit. "None of these things move me," says Paul, "neither count I my life dear unto myself, so that I might finish my course with joy." His afflictions did not move him, did not terrify him. But if death should come, what then? Why, that shall be welcome too, says he (Acts 20:24). Who is afraid of a conquered enemy, an enemy which a man sees dead and slain in the field? One that has all things ready for a dying hour sees death to be a conquered enemy, an enemy conquered by the death of Christ, and so is carried above the fear of it.

(2) Hereby the soul is enabled in a holy manner to triumph over death and even to scorn and condemn it, which is a higher conquest still. A man who has all things set right and well-ordered in the matters of the soul, he is not only carried above the terror of death, but he rides in triumph over it, as

one who divides the spoil. He can then with boldness and comfort challenge this last enemy of his and even dare it to do his worst to him: "O death, where is thy sting? O grave, where is thy victory?" says the apostle. "The sting of death is sin; and the strength of sin is the law. But thanks be to God, which giveth us the victory through our Lord Jesus Christ" (1 Cor. 15:55–57). As if he should say, "Death, you talk of a sting; but where is it? Grave, you would threaten us with victory and overthrow; but do your worst, conquer us if you can." As a man who has disarmed his enemy, thrown him upon his back, and says to him, "O Sir? Where is your sword? Where is your pistol? Where is the execution you threatened? Do your worst."

(3) Hereby the soul comes to be able solemnly to choose and desire death—yea, very much to exult and rejoice in death, as that which of an enemy is become a friend and an inlet into all happiness to him. So 2 Corinthians 5:5–6, 8: "Now he that hath wrought us for the selfsame thing is God, who also hath given unto us the earnest of the Spirit. Therefore we are always confident, knowing that, whilst we are at home in the body, we are absent from the Lord.... We are confident, I say, and willing rather to be absent from the body, and to be present with the Lord." So Philippians 1:22–23: "But if I live in the flesh, this is the fruit of my labour; yet what I shall choose I wot not. For I am in a strait betwixt two, having a desire to depart, and to be with Christ; which is far better."

Notice, he desires death, he chooses death, as that which is a friend to him and an inlet into his happiness. Such a one can say, as I have read a German divine did, when dying, "I am ready," says he, "and desire to be gone out of this life, in which all things are not only full of miseries and calamities, but, which is to be lamented, all things are full fraught with sins. I say, I desire to pass into that life in which there is no sin, no misery." Yea, more, such a one can exult and rejoice

TO BE OR BECOME AWARE OF ; LEARN TO KNOW

in death: "Lord, now lettest thou thy servant depart in peace, according to thy word: for mine eyes have seen thy salvation" (Luke 2:29–30). They are words of joy and exultation in the sight of death's approach.

The child of some tender father, being abroad at sojourn, and seeing a messenger come from his father to fetch him home—how does he exult and rejoice? "O," says he, "my father has sent for me to come home! Now I must go live with my father, to eat and drink at my father's table, to live in my father's presence, to enjoy my father's love and counsels!" And this he rejoices in and exultingly embraces the messenger. It is the very case here. The soul having all things ready, all things set right within, when death comes, it is but as a messenger to him to fetch him home to his father's house, which he can welcome and embrace with joy. "O," says he, "my Father has sent for me to come home, home to heaven, there to live immediately in His presence and upon His fullness; and now I shall be forever with my Father, now I shall ever feast my soul with my Father's love and the constant view of my Father's face. Now I shall 'see him face to face,' whom here I could never 'see but through a glass darkly.' Now I shall see and be forever in the embraces of my sweet Lord, my Lord who bled for me, who died for me, who 'trod the winepress alone for me'; now shall I enter into the 'glorious liberty of the children of God.' I have hitherto been in bondage to Satan, in bondage to my own heart, which has all along wretchedly imposed itself upon me; but now I shall enter upon the glorious liberty of the children of God. Now I shall 'partake of the inheritance of the saints in light.' Now I shall bathe my soul in the crystal streams of undefiled pleasures, running fresh along the banks of eternity at my Father's right hand. Now I shall spend a whole eternity in praises, doxologies, and hallelujahs to God and the Lamb. Now I shall have all my spots and wrinkles, my sins and sorrows done away at once. Now shall I sigh no more, and, which is infinitely better, I shall sin no more forever, no more complain of dark visions and short visits from God, no more complain of distances and alienation between Him and my soul forever. There shall be no more interruption of communion with my sweet Savior, but I shall stand in His presence and behold His face forevermore."

In a word, hereby death the king of terrors becomes the king of comforts to the soul, and a man comes to die both happily and comfortably. Some men die neither happily nor comfortably, and such is the case of all who die outside of Christ; they die in their sins, they die to be damned forever. Some die happily but not comfortably; such is the case of poor Christians dying under desertion, whose sun sets in a cloud. They die in the dark, not knowing what shall become of their souls to eternity, which yet go safe to heaven, being built upon the Rock of Ages, the Lord Jesus Christ. Some die both happily and comfortably; such is the case of all those who have all things set right between God and them, all things ready and in order before a dying hour comes. Some die presumptuously, thinking all is right and well in the matters of their souls, when indeed nothing is so; that is sad for eternity. May the Lord deliver your souls and mine from such an exit. Some die trembling or doubting, not knowing how things are with them, whether well or ill, but they fear ill; that is sad, at least for a time. May the Lord carry us above such an exit. Some (viz., well-ordered souls) die fiducially, knowing things to be right between God and them, and that is comfortable both for time and eternity. Well, then, if hereby we come to have such a glorious victory over death and the grave, it must then be a great attainment to have all things in order between God and us, and consequently greatly our concern to have things so.

Second, hereby we come to have a rich and glorious entrance ministered to us into everlasting life and glory, into heaven and blessedness. As hereby we come to be glorious conquerors over natural death, so hereby we come to have a rich and glorious entrance ministered to us into eternal life, which also carries much sweetness and blessedness in it. "And besides this, giving all diligence, add to your faith virtue; and to virtue knowledge" (2 Peter 1:5, 11). That is, grow as complete in grace as possibly you can, make sure of your salvation, make all ready in the matters of your souls. And what then? "So an entrance shall be ministered unto you abundantly into the everlasting kingdom of our Lord and Saviour Jesus Christ." And is not this a blessed attainment? Take this in three things.

(1) Hereby the soul comes to enjoy much of heaven here upon earth, much of blessedness and glory whilst on this side of blessedness and glory; then has a man an abundant entrance ministered unto him into heaven and glory, when he has much of heaven and glory given out to him here on earth, large earnest, and firstfruits. This the soul has that has all things right in the matters of his spiritual state, all things ready and in order within. Hence we read sometimes of the "earnest," and sometimes of the "firstfruits of the Spirit" (Eph. 1:14; Rom. 8:23). And the soul that is most ready has the greatest earnest and firstfruits—that is to say, the greatest beginnings of heaven here upon earth. For that which makes us ready for a dying hour is something of heaven dropped into the soul here.

(2) Hereby he comes to go triumphing from earth to heaven, to go to heaven and glory with a crown upon his head, and is not this a sweet attainment? Then has a man an abundant entrance into heaven and glory when he goes triumphing thither; when a man passes into heaven and glory, with visions there in his eye and foretastes thereof in his soul,

with a clear witness and evidence in his spirit, that he is going to possess to the fullness thereof with God and Christ forever; when a man enters into life without any rebukes from God or his own conscience, without any stumbling through doubting or unbelief. This is the happiness of such as have all things well in their souls before a dying hour comes. It is with such in death, as it was with John in the vision (Rev. 4:1). They (as it were) heard a voice from heaven saying, "Come up hither," and immediately they are in the Spirit.

So poor souls crowd into heaven through a threat of doubts and unbelief, difficulties and despondence, through many fears and temptations, insomuch that it might be truly said of them that they are "scarcely saved," as the apostle's expression is. But others go through none of these; they go triumphing, with a crown upon their head, as it were. So Paul says, "I am now ready to be offered, and the time of my departure is at hand. I have fought a good fight, I have finished my course, I have kept the faith: henceforth there is laid up for me a crown of righteousness, which the Lord, the righteous judge, shall give me at that day: and not to me only, but unto all them also that love his appearing" (2 Tim. 4:6–8). Methinks I see how his holy soul went triumphing to the throne of God and the Lamb. When "David and the House of Israel brought up the Ark of the Lord, it was with shouting, and with the sound of the trumpet," so when such a soul goes to rest, it is with a kind of shouting and triumph among the saints themselves, who all reach the same heaven and glory at last. There's a very great deal of difference in their path and in their going to that heaven and glory.

As you know, two ships may arrive at the same harbor yet with much difference as to the matter of their coming in. The one makes a change in direction to get in without much trouble, but the other arrives with her anchors lost, her sails torn and rent, her flags down, her masts broken, and the like. But the other comes in bravely, riding as it were in triumph, with her sails spread, her anchors safe, her flags flying, her trumpets sounding, and her mariners shouting. So great a difference there is in the passing of saints to heaven and blessedness. Now what an attainment must it be to go with shouting and triumph.

(3) Hereby the soul comes to be admitted to and invested with an eminent fullness of blessedness and glory with God forever, and this he has who has all right and ready in the concerns of his soul when he comes to die. Such a one receives a "full reward," as the expression is (2 John 1:8), and has much fruit abounding to his account (Phil. 4:17). O what a sweet and blessed attainment does this speak it to be, to have all in order for when a dying hour comes. Now if it be such an attainment to have things set right and in order in our souls for a dying hour, then surely it must needs be highly our concern to have things so.

CHAPTER 4

The Finality of Death

Which shows the state of men and women under death as a further evidence of this assertion.

As to have all things ready and in order when a dying hour comes is a high and glorious attainment, so such is the state and condition of men and women under death that it cannot but be highly their concern to have all things set right, all things ready in the matters of their souls, when they come to die. This I will set before you in three propositions.

The first proposition is this: that such is the state and condition of men and women under death that there is no return for them into this life anymore forever. When once a man's sun is set, it never rises more. When once a man has his part and is gone off the stage of this world, he never enters more; there is no more any part to be acted here by him. This you have in the text, "Before I go hence and be no more"—that is, no more in this world. So Job 7:7–10: "O remember that my life is wind: mine eye shall no more see good. The eye of him that hath seen me shall see me no more: thine eyes are upon me, and I am not. As the cloud is consumed and vanisheth away: so he that goeth down to the grave shall come up no more. He shall return no more to his house, neither shall his place know him any more." And again, Job 16:22: "When a few years are come, then I shall go the way whence I shall not return." All of this shows that when a man is once off the stage of this world, there is no return for him anymore.

The second proposition is this: that such is the state of men and women under death that there is nothing to be done for their souls. There is nothing to be mended that is amiss, nothing to be set in order that shall be found out of order. Death is not the time of working but of receiving the reward of our work. Death leaves us under an utter and eternal impossibility of ever doing anything for another world. Therefore, "whatsoever thy hand findeth to do," says Solomon, "do it with all thy might; for there is no work, nor device, nor knowledge, nor wisdom, in the grave whither thou goest" (Eccl. 9:10). And "I must work the works of him that sent me, while it is day: the night cometh, when no man can work," says Christ (John 9:4). Death is a state of darkness, and it deprives us of all helps, advantages, and opportunities of ever doing anything for the good of our souls. There is no repenting, no believing, no turning to God in the grave. There is no attaining pardon of sin, no getting an interest in Jesus Christ, no making our calling and election sure there. O no! These things must be done now, or they can never be done; and if they be never done, our souls are forever undone. It was an Epicurean saying of him who said, "Eat, drink, play; for after death there is no pleasure." But it would be a Christian saying to say to you, and my own soul, "Love God, pray to Him, seek His face, repent, believe, make sure of Christ; for after death none of these are to be done." They must be done here or never.

The third proposition is this: that such is the state of men and women under death that the soul is actually and irreversibly stated and concluded in its eternal condition. The soul's eternal state is absolutely fixed and unchangeably determined, without any alteration forever. It's an observation among the Schoolmen, that look what befell the angels that sinned, that in death befalls wicked men, those that are not ready for a dying hour. The angels immediately upon their sinning were stated in an irreversible condition of woe and misery. And wicked men, unready souls, immediately upon death are irreversibly stated in a like eternal condition; they are eternally sealed up under damnation. And the devils may as soon get out of those chains of eternal darkness, whereinto they are cast and in which they are locked up, being reserved unto judgment, as such persons can change or reverse that condition.

The truth is, death, whenever or wherever it comes, is as a determining thing; it concludes the soul forever under an unalterable state of life or death, of happiness or misery, for "where the tree falleth, there it shall be" (Eccl. 11:3). Hence, in death, the spirit, the soul, is said to "return unto God" (Eccl. 12:7), upon which a learned man has this observation: God (said he) receives the soul of man, when he dies, to Himself; and having received it, He delivers it either to the holy angels, that by them it might be carried to heaven, if it had been holy and good, or He delivers it to the evil angels, by them to be dragged into hell, if it hath been ungodly. Hence the apostle tells us that after death comes judgment (Heb. 9:27), by which is meant the particular judgment of every man and woman immediately upon death, which is nothing else but the stating of the soul in an eternal condition. Hence also, when Dives[1] is brought in desiring that Lazarus might "dip the tip of his finger in water to cool his tongue," the answer is made that it cannot be, for as much as there is no going for any, either from hell to heaven or from heaven to hell, because "there is a great gulf fixed" (Luke 16:26), noting the unalterableness of

---

1. The rich man in Luke 16.

that state which death sets men down in, whether happiness or misery.

Well, then, if such be the state of men and women under death, as we have heard, then surely it is highly our concern to have all ready, all in order for when a dying hour comes. Having given you thus briefly the demonstration of the point, I shall make some practical improvement of it.

CHAPTER 5

The Foolishness of Being Unprepared

Wherein sinners are convinced of their sin and folly in their neglect of this concern. With six weighty pleas or arguments to set home this conviction and awaken them to their work.

Is this indeed a concern of so much weight and moment to us? Then how great is their folly, and what enemies are they to their own souls, who live in the neglect of this great business and concern (which most men do)? God is pleased to spare—yea, wonderfully to spare—them for days, for weeks, for months, for years together, and that for this very end: that they should make themselves ready and set all right in the matters of their souls, for when a dying hour comes. But woe and alas for them! This they mind not, this they concern not themselves about, but inconsiderately live in a total neglect thereof, than which what greater folly can they be guilty of? Pray to mind what God Himself speaks in this case in Deuteronomy 32:28–29, where He says concerning Israel, "They are a nation void of counsel, neither is there any understanding in them." And what then? "O that they were wise, that they understood this, that they would consider their latter end!"

Observe here two things attested and verified by God Himself. First, that it is a point of the highest wisdom the sons of men are capable of seriously to consider their latter end—that is, to prepare for death and to set all things right in the matters of their souls so as that things may issue well with them at last and they may go off the stage of this world with comfort. Second, that not to do this is a point of the greatest folly. It does evidently argue men to be void of counsel and all true understanding. It would have been their wisdom to have considered their latter end, and their not doing it argued them to be guilty of notorious folly. These things, you may see, God Himself attests and verifies here.

What greater folly can there be than for a man to live in the neglect of that which is of so much weight and importance for him to mind as this is? Surely the greater the concern is, the greater must our folly be in the neglect thereof. Yet this is the folly that the most of men are guilty of; they mind not their latter end, their dying hour, at least not so as to make a timely provision for it. God lets them live many years, and perhaps they rejoice in them all; but they forget the days of darkness, which are many. They regard not the state of their souls, nor how things stand between God and them in reference to another world. O that this were not the folly of too many of us, who profess the belief of another life, a future state! We live and enjoy good, but we "put far away the evil day," as those are said to do in Amos 6:3. God spares us time after time, but no provision do we make for a dying hour.

O how many of us have never yet set anything right in the matters of our souls, anything in order for when the time comes, when we are to go hence and be no more, that have scarce ever had yet one serious thought of death, judgment, or eternity, nor make the least tittle of provision for them? And what shall I say to such? I would (if God saw good) awaken them out of their folly and convince them of it. In order to which, I would plead a little with them in six particulars.

(1) Must we not all go hence? Solomon tells us, There is "a time to be born, and a time to die" (Eccl. 3:2). And the one is as sure as the other; as sure as we have had a time to be born, so surely we shall have a time to die, and the living know it. "The living know that they shall die," says Solomon (Eccl. 9:5). Indeed, they may well know it. For not only the experience of between five and six thousand years tells them so, but it is what is appointed, what is infallibly determined by the unchangeable law and decrees of heaven (Heb. 9:27). Nor can anything whatever exempt us from the stroke of death.

Youthful strength and vigor can't do it. For young men die as well as old; strong men die as well as weak. "One dieth in his full strength," says the Holy Ghost, "being wholly at ease and quiet. His breasts are full of milk, and his bones are moistened with marrow" (Job 21:23–24).

Worldly pomp and greatness can't do it. For great men die as well as mean men; rich men die as well as poor men. "Where is the house of the prince?" (says the Holy Ghost). Answer is made, "Yet shall he be brought to the grave, and shall remain in the tomb. The clods of the valley shall be sweet unto him, and every man shall draw after him, as there are innumerable before him" (Job 21:28, 32–33). So in Psalm 49:16–19: "Be not thou afraid when one is made rich, when the glory of his house is increased; for when he dieth he shall carry nothing away: his glory shall not descend after him. Though while he lived he blessed his soul…. He shall go to the generation of his fathers; they shall never see light."

Human wisdom and policy can't do it, for wise men die as well as fools. So Psalm 49:10: "Wise men die, likewise the fool"; yes, in many respects, wise men die as the fool (Eccl. 2:16). Pray what is become of all the wise men and great politicians who have lived in former ages? Truly the clods of the valley cover them.

Spiritual gifts and graces can't do it. For good men die as well as bad, holy men as well as wicked men. "The righteous perisheth, and no man layeth it to heart: and merciful men are taken away" (Isa. 57:1).

Eminence of place and service can't do it. "Your fathers, where are they? and the prophets, do they live for ever?" (Zech. 1:5). What higher place than to be a prophet, to be an ambassador for God? And yet such die. Nothing (you see) can exempt us from the stroke of death. Why then should we neglect to prepare for it? I will close this head with a saying I have read in one of the ancients: "What among human affairs," says he, "is more certain than death? What more uncertain than the hour of death? Death has no compassion for poverty, neither does it reverence greatness; it spares no gender, no manners, no age, only it seems to come in at the gate upon old men; but craftily it steals in upon young ones."

(2) Does not death hasten upon us all? As we must all die, so death hastens apace upon us; every step we take is a step toward death and the grave. So we find in Ecclesiastes 9:10. "Our whole life is," as one well observes upon that place, "nothing else but a journey towards death and the grave." Whether we sleep or wake, eat or drink, trade or travel, pray or play, we are still hastening to the grave. A dying hour hastens upon all, and how fast does it hasten upon us? Faster than the weaver's shuttle does to the end of the web. "My days," says Job, "are swifter than a weaver's shuttle" (Job 7:6). How fast does it hasten upon us? As fast, yea, faster, than a post hastens to the end of his stage, or a swift ship to the harbor under the advantage of wind and tide, or the swift flying eagle to the prey. "Now my days are swifter than a post," says Job. "They flee away, they see no good. They are passed away as the swift ships: as the eagle that hasteth to the prey" (Job 9:25–26). How fast does it hasten upon us? So fast as that for ought we

know, it will be upon us before we see the light of another day. "Thou fool, this night thy soul shall be required of thee" (Luke 12:20). How fast does it hasten upon us? So fast as that for ought we know, it may be upon us the next hour—yea, the next moment. "They spend their days in wealth, and in a moment go down to the grave" (Job 21:13). To be sure, it will be upon us speedily, and it may be upon us suddenly. I pray consider, what are we? And what is our life? Wind, as in Job 7:7: "O remember that my life is wind." A handbreadth, as in Psalm 39:5: "Behold, thou hast made my days as an hand-breadth; and mine age is as nothing before thee." A declining shadow, as in Psalm 102:11: "My days are like a shadow that declineth; and I am withered like grass." A flower of the field which is withered and gone with the wind: "As for man, his days are as grass: as a flower of the field, so he flourisheth. For the wind passeth over it, and it is gone; and the place thereof shall know it no more" (Ps. 103:15–16). And again, "All flesh is grass, and all the goodliness thereof is as the flower of the field: the grass withereth, the flower fadeth: because the spirit of the LORD bloweth upon it: surely the people is grass" (Isa. 40:6–7). Vanity and a shadow: "Man is like to vanity: his days are as a shadow that passeth away" (Ps. 144:4), "a vapour, that appeareth for a little time, and then vanisheth away" (James 4:14). O how soon may one, or another, or all of us be among the dead? How soon may death approach us?

(3) What infinite mercy is it that God has spared us so long and still does spare us to set things right, to make all ready for a dying hour? O my friends, how great is the sparing mercy of God toward us? We have had some ten, some twenty, some thirty, some forty, some fifty, some sixty years in the world, and still God spares us; still He lets us live and enjoy good. And why all this, think you? Surely to set things right in our souls, to make ready for a dying hour, and shall we yet neglect it?

God forbid! Oh, think a little, I beseech you, with yourselves, how long since the grave might have swallowed us up and the bottomless pit have shut its mouth upon us? How long will it be before time and days have come to an end with us, and our souls are placed in a miserable eternity? But still God spares us, and we are yet in the land of the living, with a door of mercy and grace yet opened unto us; at least a possibility is left us of knowing the things of our peace in our day, of making provision for death and eternity. O what a mercy is this! I would fain a little quicken both you and myself by this consideration. In order thereunto, let me plead a little more particularly with you.

(i) Consider how long God has spared and does spare you, beyond what He does and has for thousands and ten thousands of others. God does not spare all at that rate which He has spared and does still spare us. Alas! how many thousands are there now free among the dead, who came into being long since we did? Their hourglass is run out, their sun is set, their day is over, their hopes and expectations are all at an end. Their souls are stated in an eternal condition, a condition that will admit of neither change nor period forever, and yet we are spared still. They came into the world long after us and are gone into eternity long before us. Yea, how many are there that never arrived to the one half of those years that we have arrived unto? Their sun has set in the morning. How many of us have outlived our yokefellows, our children, our servants, our friends and acquaintances? Yet we stand our ground. And all this that we might prepare for a dying hour. This patience of God should lead us to repentance (Rom. 2:4). O that it might do so!

(ii) Consider how much we have provoked God and what advantage we have given Him in justice to be against us. I would say here, as Christ speaks in another case, "Suppose ye that these Galilaeans [whose blood Pilate mingled with their sacrifices] were sinners above all the Galilaeans, because they suffered such things? I tell you, Nay: but, except ye repent, ye shall all likewise perish. Or those eighteen, upon whom the tower in Siloam fell, and slew them, think ye that they were sinners above all men that dwelt in Jerusalem? I tell you, Nay; but, except ye repent, ye shall all likewise perish" (Luke 13:2–5).

So say I here, suppose you that those who are gone down to the gates of the grave and the bars of death before us were greater sinners than we? I tell you nay, but except we repent, we must all likewise perish. We have sinned as well as they, and possibly in many regards more than they. To be sure, we have all over and over deserved long since to have been covered with the shadow of the night of eternal darkness. O how has the patience of God been tried, and His longsuffering tested by us! What burden have we been to His soul! Some of us have cause to think that we have been as great a burden to God as the most that have ever lived. How justly may the blessed God complain of many of us that we have made Him to serve with our sins, and wearied Him with our iniquities, as He did them of old (Isa. 43:24); that we have broken His heart with our whorish heart, whereby we have departed from Him (Ezek. 6:9); that our sins have pressed Him down as a cart is pressed that is full of sheaves (Amos 2:13)?

Alas, alas! How have we wallowed in our pollution and acted out the enmity and rebellion of our natures against Him? How have we rejected His Word, resisted His Spirit, despised His grace, trampled upon His Son, refused many and many an offer of love and many a sweet call and a blessed invitation to come to the marriage supper of the Lamb? And yet that He should still spare us. O what mercy is this? In 1 Peter 3:20 we read that "the longsuffering of God waited in the days of Noah." And truly, my beloved, it waits as much in our days,

and our provocations be as many and as high against Him as
theirs of that generation were. O friends, why are we not in
hell? Why are we not sealed and shut up among the damned?
Why have we one still more, one offer more, one season of
grace more? Verily, it is all rich mercy. O that it might lead us
to repentance!

(iii) Consider how sad it had been with us had the Lord
taken that advantage against us which we have over and over
given Him. Suppose, my beloved, God had not spared us but
had cut us off, as He might long since; what now would become
of us? And where now had we been? Had you died of such and
such a sickness you have been in, when possibly a sentence of
death was passed upon you, where and how miserable had you
been? Had you not been now in flames eternally separated
from God and Christ, being godless and Christless? Have you
not now to fear you had been in as irrecoverable a condition
as the devils themselves are in, sealed up under wrath and
condemnation, past all hopes and possibility of mercy forever?
"Whither had I gone," says Augustine, "if then [speaking of
the time he was in his sins] I had gone hence? Whither had I
gone but into the flames, and into eternal torments, answerable to my sins?" May not we say the like? But, blessed be God,
it is yet time and season with me and you; we are spared to this
hour, that we might provide for death and eternity. O friends,
suppose you or I were now among the damned; suppose we
were as they are, sealed up under wrath and separated from
God, left under an utter impossibility of ever seeing His face;
how sad then would our condition be? Why, thus it might have
been with us! O what mercy is it then that God has spared us
and does spare us as He does? And how should it awaken us
to our work?

(iv) Consider how much more sad it may and will yet be
with us in case we provide not for a dying hour. Truly, the

longer God spares us, if we answer not His end in His sparing mercy, the more answerable shall we be forever. It will be sad to perish at all, but it will be doubly sad to perish under the longsuffering of God, under the rebuke of much goodness and long patience. O to have many days' and many years' patience and goodness come in to witness against a man at last. How sad will this be! Think of and seriously lay to heart that Scripture, Romans 2:4–5: "Despisest thou the riches of his goodness and forbearance and longsuffering; not knowing that the goodness of God leadeth thee to repentance? But after thy hardness and impenitent heart treasurest up unto thyself wrath against the day of wrath and revelation of the righteous judgment of God." Every day which God in His patience affords us, if we be not led to repentance, is a day of treasuring up wrath, heaping up to ourselves wrath against the day of wrath, when wrath shall come upon us to the utmost. Well, think then what a mercy it is that God spares you as He does and what an obligation this sparing mercy of His is upon you, to set all things right in the matters of your souls for when a dying hour comes.

(4) Are you sure that those helps and advantages which you enjoy now to further you in your work will always last and be enjoyed by you? Suppose, my beloved, that God should yet spare you and prolong your days in the land of the living. Yet, O how soon may all your helps and advantages to further you in this great work be withdrawn from you! Now, blessed be God, you enjoy many blessed helps and advantages for your furtherance in this great work, but how quickly may they all be gone!

(i) How soon may the reproofs, the counsels, the holy examples of your godly friends, ministers, and relations be withdrawn from you? Now you enjoy the loving reproofs, the wholesome counsels, the holy examples of such and such friends and relations; one reproves you for sin, another

quickens you to duty; one advises you against the world and
carnal pleasures; another persuades you to close with Christ
and walk with God, to pursue after heaven and eternal life;
one woos and beseeches you, another charges and commands
you to labor and know God and to live to Him, to provide
for another life, and they all show you the path of life. They
tread the way to heaven in your sight, all which are great helps
and advantages to further you in this great concern of yours.
But how soon may all these be withdrawn? Your friends, your
ministers, your relations will speedily be lodged in the dust,
and you shall never have a word of reproof, a word of counsel,
a word of quickening, a word of encouragement, or a pattern
of faith and holiness set before you by them anymore forever,
which would be a dreadful thing. Now the godly father, mother,
yokefellow, master, friend, and acquaintance is plying you with
counsels and instructions for the good of your soul; tomorrow
it may be, he or she goes down to the gates of the grave, and
then there will be no more of this life forever.

(ii) How soon may the Word and ordinances of God,
which you now enjoy, be withdrawn from you? Now you enjoy
the Word and ordinances of God. You go from ordinance to
ordinance; you have line upon line, precept upon precept, as
it is in Isaiah 28:10. Yea, let me tell you, you see and hear these
things which many prophets and righteous men have desired
to see and hear but saw and heard them not (Matt. 13:17).
O how is light and immortality brought to light to you? How
is the way of salvation made plain and manifest before you?
What glorious discoveries? What blessed revelations? What
sweet and frequent tenders of Christ are made to you? How
freely are you called to the marriage supper of the Lamb? How
lovingly does Christ invite you to Himself? How kindly does
He stand knocking at the door of your souls? Oh, my beloved,
I may now say to you as Paul to the Corinthians, "Behold,

now is the accepted time; behold, now is the day of salvation"
(2 Cor. 6:2). O what helps and advantages are these? But how
soon may they all be gone? How soon may the Word of God
be withdrawn? How soon may your light be put out and your
souls left in darkness, not knowing whither to go? Remember
that word of Christ, and lay it to heart: "Yet a little while is
the light with you. Walk while ye have the light, lest darkness
come upon you: for he that walketh in darkness knoweth not
whither he goeth. While ye have light, believe in the light, that
ye may be the children of light" (John 12:35–36). It is a great
question whether we may not lose gospel ordinances and all,
and where are we then?

(iii) How soon may the motions and striving of the Spirit of
God be withdrawn from you? Now you have the motions and
striving of the Spirit of God in you and with you; He "moves
upon the face of the water" in your souls; He moves and strives
in and by the Word and ordinances, mercies, and afflictions.
Now you have enlightening, and then you have quickening
influences from Him. Now He shows you your work, and then
He tenders you His assistance. Now He discovers the odiousness of sin to you, and then He displays the beauty, sweetness,
and excellency of Christ and holiness before you. But alas!
how soon may all this be at an end? Think of that terrible
word, "My spirit shall not always strive with man" (Gen. 6:3).
God may possibly the next day—yea, the next hour—say to
His Spirit concerning one or another of us, "Let him alone,
strive no more with him, move no more in him, convince him
no more, persuade him no more, draw and allure him no
more; he is addicted to his lusts and to this world. Let him
alone; he has no mind to heaven, no desire to make any provision for another world. Let him alone; he is unwilling to see
beyond time to eternity; he is given to his carnal pleasures. Let
him alone; he has a resisting, gainsaying spirit. Let him alone."

O how soon these and all other advantages you now enjoy may be withdrawn—who knows? You have all these together in one Scripture, which I desire you to lay to heart: "And when he was come near, he beheld the city [speaking of Jerusalem], and wept over it, saying, If thou hadst known, even thou, at least in this thy day, the things which belong unto thy peace! but now they are hid from thine eyes" (Luke 19:41–42). They had a day herein they did enjoy the things of their peace; they might and should have improved their duty and the things of their peace by securing their eternal state. But they neglected it, and now all these are withdrawn from them; the joy of the whole earth to weep over them, so woeful, miserable, and deplorable He saw their condition to be. And how sad will it be with you if once Christ should come to say over you that dismal word, "Now they are hid from your eyes!"

(5) Is it an easy matter, think you, to set things right in your souls and to make all things ready for a dying hour? Suppose, my beloved, that you should live yet many days, and withal, your helps and advantages for the good of your souls shall be continued to you. Yet is it an easy work which you have to do? And shall you have time and days to spare? Believe it, all will be little enough to set things right, to make things ready for a dying hour. Pray consider with me these few things as to this.

(i) Consider in what a woeful disorder all things are at present with you and how utterly unready you are for a dying hour. I will give you what the Scriptures state of your case. You are "dead in trespasses and sins"; under whole loads and mountains of scarlet crimson guilt; "without Christ, without hope, without God in the world, alienated, and enemies in your minds, by wicked works"—yea, enmity itself against God and Christ; full of sin, both within and without, and nothing but sin, having no good dwelling in you; void of all grace, all true spiritual life; under the power and predominancy of lust, "serving divers lusts and pleasures, and carried captive by the devil at his will"; closely glued to and deeply in love with this world; ignorant of God and of the great mystery of the Father and of Christ, at least having no saving knowledge of them; no savor of heaven, no relish of spiritual things in your souls; wallowing in your blood and gore, being filthy and "abominable, to every good work reprobate"; the heart strongly averse from God and all good, and vigorously bent to sin and vanity; nothing of heaven within, but full of hell, full of the spirit and image of the devil; under the law of sin, strangers to the law of grace; no union with Christ, no oil in the vessel; "poor, miserable, blind, and naked," at most, "having but the form, and denying the power of Godliness." This is your condition. O what disorders are these! And what an unready posture are you in for death and eternity.

♦ (ii) Consider how great a thing it is to be ready for death, ready indeed, and to have all things set right and in order for when a dying hour comes, and how much is required in order to be ready. It is a great saying of a holy man: "No one," says he, "can joyfully welcome death, but he that has been long composing his spirit and making ready for it." O my beloved, to be indeed ready to quit the world, to go into the divine presence—the great, the holy, the glorious presence of God—to be ready to enter upon the beatifical vision, to possess a mansion in the Father's house, to join with a heavenly host of angels and spirits of just men made perfect in eternal praising, admiring, and adoring of Father, Son, and Holy Ghost. Believe it, this is a great thing, and great things are requisite thereunto. This calls for a near union with Christ, a firm peace with God, clear evidences for heaven; for much grace and holiness, much heavenliness and spirituality of mind, much weanedness from this world, much holy deadness to sin, self, and the creature; much victory over corruption; much soul-cleansing;

much purity of heart and affection; much diligence and faithfulness in duties. And, my beloved, are these little things, or things easily to be accomplished and attained unto? The Scripture, speaking of these things, calls upon us to strive (Luke 13:24), to give all diligence in the pursuit of them (2 Peter 1:5, 10), to manage and dispatch them with fear and trembling (Phil. 2:12)—all which tells us that they are great things and not easily to be accomplished and attained unto. Therefore, we had need look after this and neglect no longer.

(iii) Consider what obstacles and hindrances, difficulties and oppositions you must expect to meet withal in your minding and managing this work; not only is the work itself great but you must also expect many obstacles and hindrances, much difficulty and opposition in the managing of it. You must expect obstacles and oppositions from the devil; he is the enemy of souls. And you must expect that he will make use of all his wiles, methods, and devices, all his craft and cunning, all his artifices, and that he will stir up all his wrath and malice against you. He is your enemy, and he is a subtle enemy, a potent enemy, an indefatigable enemy, an enemy who always goes about "seeking whom he may devour" (1 Peter 5:8). You must expect obstacles and oppositions from the world too, from the men of the world, from the things of the world, from the smiles of the world, from the frowns of the world. The world is your enemy as well as the devil. So much is intimated in 1 John 5:4. And you must expect opposition from it. The men of the world will discourage you; the things of the world will divert you; the troubles of the world will mightily depress you; the enjoyments of the world will miserably ensnare and entangle you. The world is of a marvelous bewitching, ensnaring, and entangling nature. It is indeed opposite to God and all goodness and so to the whole interest of our souls. "The friendship of the world is enmity with God" (James 4:4). The world will plead for and take up your time, your strength, your thoughts. O the hindrance that the world is to thousands, and ten thousands, to the work in their souls; truly this ruins multitudes forever. This ruined him whom we read of in Matthew 19:22. And, says Paul, "Demas hath forsaken me, having loved this present world" (2 Tim. 4:10).

You must expect obstacles and hindrances also from your own hearts—yea, from them above all others. "The heart," the Holy Ghost tells us, "is deceitful above all things, and desperately wicked" (Jer. 17:9). And who of us does at all observe it, and in the working of it, does not find it to be so? Now it will openly oppose you, then it will secretly seduce you and ensnare you. Now it will carry you off and draw you back from God and duty (Heb. 3:12). Then it will turn you aside to sin and vanity (Isa. 44:20). Now it will divert you from duty, then it will make you dead and slothful in duty. It is indeed wholly set against all that is good, and it has a thousand ways to hinder you in your great work.

And you must expect that it will do its utmost to hinder you. This is a close enemy. It is always at hand; there is no end of its opposition, till life itself ends. One of the ancients (I remember) breaks out into a sad exclamation against his own heart, thus: "My heart," says he, "is a wicked heart, a vain heart, a roving, and wandering heart. My mind is exceeding light, inconstant, a vagabond, and a fugitive, that changes itself into all shapes; it will, and it will not; it is like a leaf moved and carried about with the wind. My vain and importunate heart hails me now to the market, and then to strifes and brawlings; now to feasting, and then to impure lusts; now the flesh is inflamed with sordid titillations, then the mind is defiled with filthy cogitations." And who of us may not make the same complaint? Yes, such is the enmity and opposition of our own hearts against heaven, and the things of heaven, that many times when we most resolve and set ourselves to follow God, and to pursue the work of our souls, then they set us most back. It was a great speech of that same ancient Father: "This," says he, "is my daily exercise, with my whole strength I bend to Thee, and would mount up to God and heaven, but by how much the more strongly I endeavor to come up to Thee, but so much the more powerfully I am cast into the earth, into myself, and even under myself, captivated to my lusts."

And so it is often with us. Obstacles, then, and oppositions must be expected by us on all hands, and we had need therefore the more to awaken to our work. It is true, if you will engage in good earnest in the work of your souls, your helps and encouragements will be greater than your obstacles and discouragements; you will have more with you than against you. You will have God with you, and Christ with you, and the Comforter with you, and all the graces of the covenant with you; be encouraged, therefore, to set upon soul work. Now lay all these things together and see if it be an easy matter to make ready for a dying hour; and if it be not, why should we neglect it? Why should we delay any longer?

(6) How terrible will death be to you, and what a dreadful change will it make with you, in case you still neglect to make ready for it! Suppose, my beloved, you go on in the neglect of this great concern, "putting far from you the evil day." What, think you, will the issue of it be? Will not death be most terrible to you when you shall be called to conflict with it? Will it not make a dreadful change with you? Surely it will. Death to an unready soul—what will it be? It will be the period of all his mercies, of all his comforts, of all his hopes. For such a one receives all his good things in this life, before death comes (Luke 16:25); it will be the sending of him to his own place, the cutting him down as fuel for everlasting burnings. It will be (as a worthy divine speaks) "as the taking up of a draw-bridge,

and the pulling up of the flood gate of God's eternal wrath, to let in the deluge of it upon his soul forever." It will be a change to him. But what change will it be? Surely a very sad one.

(i) A change from earth to hell, and is not this a sad change? "The wicked shall be turned into hell, and all the nations that forget God" (Ps. 9:17). And we read of the rich man (who was unready for death) that being dead, he was in hell (Luke 16:23).

(ii) A change from light to darkness, and is not that a sad change? The Holy Ghost, speaking of such a one, tells us God shall drive him out of light into darkness, and chase him out of the world (Job 18:18). Here wicked men enjoy the light of creature comforts, but God will drive them out of these into the darkness of eternal misery, into "outer darkness" (Matt. 25:30), into "blackness of darkness" (Jude 13).

(iii) A change from pleasure to pain, from delight to torment. A sad change it is from pleasure and delight in sin to pain and torment for sin (Luke 16:23). Here the soul sports himself in the pleasures and delights of sin, and he thinks he can never have enough; but then there will be an end of all those pleasures and delights, and nothing but pain, torment, and vexation will succeed them.

(iv) A change from the offers of grace to the revelation of wrath. "Shall thy lovingkindness be declared in the grave? or thy faithfulness in destruction?" (saith the psalmist in Ps. 88:11). True, in 1 Peter 3:19–20 we read of Christ's preaching by the Spirit to the spirits in prison—that is, to souls in hell. But mark, when was it that he preached to them? Not when in prison, but in the days of Noah, when they lived in the world. There is never an offer of grace and love made to souls in the grave; while life lasts, the soul hears the joyful sound. And Oh, the sweet offers, the gracious tenders, the loving invitations that are made to him in Christ, of grace, of eternal life and love! Oh, the wooing, the melting, the entreating, the alluring of divine love to and over the soul! But when death comes, farewell all these, farewell all the sweet offers of Christ and all the blessed motions of the Spirit; then there's nothing but wrath revealed. Wrath shall come on the neglected soul to the uttermost (1 Thess. 2:16).

(v) A change from fair probabilities to utter impossibilities of life and salvation—a sad change still. Now, and not here-after (2 Cor. 6:2). Now there is a fair probability for the worst of sinners to be saved. If they will look after salvation, and mind their eternal concerns, Christ is both able and willing to save. To save was the end of His coming into the world and of all He did and suffered here (1 Tim. 1:15). Now they are besought and entreated to be reconciled to God (2 Cor. 5:19–20), but when death comes, that changes these fair probabilities into utter impossibilities of life and salvation. Therefore, mark: "Now," says the apostle "is the day of salvation"—that is, now while life lasts and while the gospel is preached.

(vi) A change from hope to despair, a sad change indeed. We read that "the hypocrite's hope shall perish" (Job 8:13) and that "the expectation of the wicked shall perish" (Prov. 10:28). Whether men be open sinners or close hypocrites, their hopes at last shall all fail and turn to despair—despair of ever seeing God or enjoying the least tittle or iota of good forever.

Thus, death will be terrible to you, and make a dreadful change with you, in case you neglect to make ready for its coming; it will affright you as bad as the handwriting upon the wall did that proud king (Dan. 5:5–6), which made his counte-nance change, his thoughts to trouble him, and the joints of his loins to be loosed and his knees to smite one against another. O when death comes, and you shall be found unready, how will your countenance change, and your joints be loosened, your thoughts troubled, and your heart tremble within you? In a word, I will say to you, as the prophet spoke of old, "What will ye do in the day of visitation…to whom will ye flee for help?" (Isa. 10:3). When death comes, what will you do? Which way will you look? Will there be any hope, any help, any refuge for your souls to flee unto? Alas! There will be none. Will you then run to the mercies of God and cry, "Lord, Lord"? Alas! It will be in vain, He will then say unto you, "I know you not" (Matt. 25:11–12). Will you then labor to get grace and pardon? Alas! It will be too late; then the door will be shut against you (Matt. 25:10). Will you then desire others to spare you some of their oil? Alas! That will be a vain thing; they will tell you they have but enough for themselves (Matt. 25:9). Will you then plead your gifts and services for Christ? Alas! It will be to no purpose, unless you have done the main work; notwith-standing all your gifts and services, He will send you away with the workers of iniquity (Matt. 7:22–23). Will you call upon the rocks and mountains to cover you from the wrath of Him that sits upon the throne? Alas! It will be in vain (Rev. 6:16).

O sinner! When you shall see yourself launching out into the great ocean of eternity and God shall, as it were, say to you, by the mouth of your own conscience, "Well now, time and days are at an end with you, and will never dawn more; what have you done for your soul? What provision have you made for another world? Is Christ yours? Have you gotten your sins pardoned, and the like?" When it shall be thus, I say, what will you then do, and whither will you then look? How will you then cry out, "Undone, undone, I am lost forever! My day is ended, and my work is still to do! Woe is me, what a God, a Christ, a heaven, a blessedness, a glory have I willfully and foolishly lost?" Truly you, and such as you, are the only persons whose death will be truly lamentable. I remember a saying I have read in one of the ancients: "They," says he, "are to be bewailed in their death whom the devils drag away to the torments of the infernal pit, not they whom the holy angels do conduct to the joys of paradise; they are to be bewailed who after death are by the devils turned into hell, and not they who by the angels are placed or set down in heaven." O that these things might convince you of your folly and awaken your souls, and that so as yet to know the things of your peace in your day and the time of your visitation!

CHAPTER 6

Prepare Yourself Now!

Being a call to all, good and bad, saints and sinners, to address themselves to the great work of making all ready for a dying hour.

What is the language of this? Verily, it calls aloud upon all, good and bad, saints and sinners, to make it our great business to set all things right in the matters of our souls and make all ready for a dying hour. And oh that we would make this improvement of this great truth and of God's sparing goodness to us! He spares us, and why does He spare us but that we should set all things right and make all things ready? O that we would now fall in with the end and design of God herein, making it our great care and business in time to provide for eternity, in life to make ready for death. Some of you, I verily believe, are about this work, and the Lord prosper you in it. You know you were born for eternity, and you do endeavor to live for eternity. Your great work in time is to make provision for a blessed eternity. O happy souls that you are! Others of us, and those by far the most (I fear), are utterly negligent in this business; death and eternity are little minded by us, but we are in a sleepy, drowsy, secure spirit, and to such His truth speaks in a language much like the ship master to Jonah: "What meanest thou, O sleeper?

arise, call upon thy God, if so be that God will think upon us, that we perish not" (Jonah 1:6).

So what mean you, O you sleepy, drowsy souls! Arise, make ready for a dying hour; set all things right, all things in order in your spiritual concerns, lest death come upon you unawares; and to such of us I would say, as God did by the prophet to Hezekiah, "Set thine house in order: for thou shalt die, and not live" (Isa. 38:1). So say I to you, set your hearts in order, your spiritual concerns in order; make all even between God and you, for you shall shortly die and not live; you shall shortly go hence and be no more, and why should we not all do so? If you are to change your condition in the world, how careful and solicitous are you to have all things ready and in order for that change? Why, my beloved, you are shortly to pass under the great and last change, a change from time to eternity, and will you have no care, no solicitude to make ready for that change? If you are to take a journey, though a few miles, or to make a voyage into a strange land, how are you concerned to have all things ready, all things in a prepared posture in order thereunto? And, my beloved, should not you be more concerned to make ready for your great journey, your last and great voyage? You are making a journey, a voyage out of time into eternity; you are launching forth into the great ocean. And what, nothing in order, nothing ready, nothing set right in order thereunto? That is strange! If you have some great business, a business of more than ordinary importance to be done, or a suit at law to be tried or determined, O how close do you follow it? And should you not be as careful and diligent to prepare and set all things right for the great business of your souls in another world? Have you any business, any concern of greater importance to you than the concern of your souls and eternity? If you are to appear before some earthly judge, especially if it be about a matter that concerns your life, O how thoughtful are you to have all things ready and in order in reference thereunto? And should not you be as thoughtful and solicitous to make all ready, and to set all right, in order to your appearing before the Judge of all the earth, and that about a matter which concerns the life of your souls, about a matter of eternal life or death?

Well, what shall I say? Will you set about this great business, this great concern? Or is it all one with you, whether you live or die, are saved or damned to eternity? God yet spares you, blessed be His name; will you not set all right before you go hence and be no more? Sinners, will you set about this great business? Your work is wholly yet to do, though it may be your day is far spent, your glass is almost run, your sun near setting, and all your work to do. Oh, it is high time for you to awake out of sleep, unless you mean to sleep the sleep of eternal death. Saints, will you set about this great blessedness while God spares you? You have done somewhat, but there is much more yet to be done; there is much out of order yet in your souls. Grace weak (it may be), corruption strong, peace broken, evidences blurred and blotted, unbelief powerful within you, the heart much estranged from God, little suitableness to heaven in your spirits, and the like; will you now labor to "recover strength"? How many of us may complain as that holy man St. Bernard once did? "I am ashamed to live because I am so unprofitable; and I am afraid to die because I am so unprepared."

Surely this truth concerns the best of us all. And if we understand ourselves, we cannot but know it; the Lord help us to know it effectually. And if after all you would indeed address this great work and business, then I have several great and weighty directions to propound to you for your help therein, of which some are more general, and some are more particular, and I would speak of each distinctly.

CHAPTER 7

Consider Death, Life, Eternity, Delay, and Prayer

Wherein are propounded several general directions in order to a thorough preparation of soul for a dying hour.

First, would you indeed set all things right to your souls, make all ready for a dying hour? Then in your most prosperous and flourishing state here, maintain a frequent and serious remembrance of death and the grave upon your spirits. "If a man live many years," says Solomon, "and rejoice in them all; yet let him remember the days of darkness; for they shall be many" (Eccl. 11:8). By the days of darkness here we are to understand death and the state of death, the abode of our bodies in the grave, which is a "land of darkness" and where "the light is as darkness" (Job 10:21–22). Now, says he, though a man live many years and rejoice in them all—that is, though a man live long and prosperously, long and joyfully—yet let him remember death and the grave, the future state.

It is true, there are other days of darkness which we are subject to in this world and should be remembered by us: days of outward darkness, the darkness of outward trouble and affliction, and days of inward darkness, the darkness of spiritual distress and dereliction. And indeed it is of marvelous use to us in our prosperity to remember these days of darkness, but especially we should remember death and the grave! We should carry a living remembrance of these days of darkness daily upon us; and indeed our not remembering these days of darkness is one great cause why we are so unready for death and the grave as we are. When we are in the midst of our enjoyments, and the streams run pleasantly about us, we are too apt to forget these days of darkness; we are so taken with our earthly comforts that we are loathe to think of death and eternity, putting "far away the evil day," as those in their enjoyments did (Amos 6:3). And therefore, when these days come, they find us so unready, and our spiritual concernments so discomposed, as usually they do. But, my beloved, as ever you would have all right and in order in your poor souls for when a dying hour comes, let me recommend this to you as one special help: maintain a deep and frequent remembrance of death and the grave upon your spirits; remember the days of darkness, and that especially these two ways.

(1) Remember them so as to have them much in your meditation. Be much and frequent in the contemplation of death and the grave. This the Holy Ghost calls a "considering our latter end" and withal mentions as a business of great importance to us (Deut. 32:29). To consider is to revolve a thing in our minds and to keep it much in our thoughts and meditations. And thus we should consider our latter end and remember the days of darkness. This is what the saints of old have been much conversant in; they were much and frequent in the thoughts and meditations of death, as I might instance in the good old patriarchs, Job, David, and others. And it is what does marvelously conduce to our preparation for it. "The meditation of death," says one, "is life." It is that which greatly promotes our spiritual life; therefore, walk much among the tombs and converse much and frequently with the thoughts of a dying hour.

(2) Remember them so as to have them daily in your expectation. In the midst of all your enjoyments, expect death's approach daily. This is called a waiting for our change: "All the days of my appointed time will I wait, till my change come" (Job 14:14). And we are commanded to wait for the coming of our Lord as that which lies in the directest tendency to the exactest readiness and preparations for His coming (Luke 12:36). "Expect death every hour," says one, "for it is every hour approaching you. In the morning, when you rise, think with yourself, this may be the last day. In the evening, when you lie down, think with yourself, this may be the last night I may ever have in this world. I know not when my Lord may come, whether in the morning, or in the evening, at midnight, or at the cock crowing. Therefore I will be always expecting His coming." Woe and alas for us! We are apt to talk of many years to come, as he did (Luke 12:19), whereas we should live in the expectation of death every moment. Thus let us consider the days of darkness; it will marvelously conduce to the preparation of the soul for them. The meditation and expectation of death will conduce much (among others) to these four things.

(i) It will conduce much to our humbling and self-debasing. "Let a man own himself to be a mortal," says Augustine, "and pride will, it must down!" And "Think frequently of death," says another, "and you will easily bring down your proud heart." Hence also the consideration of death is often in Scripture mentioned by the Holy Ghost as an argument to make us humble: "Dust thou art, and unto dust shalt thou return" (Gen. 3:19, as elsewhere).

(ii) It will conduce much to the weaning of our hearts from this world and the loosening of them from the things here below. "The time is short," says the apostle. What then? "It remaineth, that both they that have wives be as though they had none; and they that weep, as though they wept not;

and they that rejoice, as though they rejoiced not; and they that buy, as though they possessed not; and they that use this world, as not abusing it: for the fashion of this world passeth away" (1 Cor. 7:29–31). He mentions the shortness of time, as that the meditation and expectation whereof has the directest tendency in it to wean and loosen the heart from all things here below. And indeed (as St. Bernard has it), "he easily contemns all things, who looks upon himself as dying daily."

(iii) It will conduce much to engaging the heart to heaven, and the things of heaven, to a serious pursuit of a blessed eternity. So we find in Hebrews 11:13: "These all died in faith," says the apostle, "not having received the promises, but having seen them afar off, and were persuaded of them, and embraced them, and confessed that they were strangers and pilgrims on the earth"; that is, they were apprehensive they had but a little time to stay here. And what then? "They seek a better country"—that is, a heavenly one. The apprehension they had of their departure hence quickened them unto earnest desires and pursuits after the better country, the heavenly land; and indeed one great reason why we breathe no more and press no more after heaven and a blessed eternity is because we so seldom remember these days of darkness.

(iv) It will conduce much to the quickening of the heart to duty and to diligence and faithfulness therein. Christ Himself made use of it for this end: "I must work the works of him that sent me, while it is day: the night cometh, when no man can work" (John 9:4). Peter also, that holy apostle, made use of it to that end. "I will not be negligent," says he, to do so and so in the way of my duty, as "knowing that shortly I must put off this my tabernacle" (2 Peter 1:12, 14). This consideration of the near approach of his death quickened him to his work and duty. And the Scripture propounds it, as that which has a tendency to this thing. "Whatsoever thy hand findeth to do, do it with thy might," says Solomon, "for there is no work, nor device, nor knowledge, nor wisdom, in the grave, whither thou goest" (Eccl. 9:10). He propounds the consideration of our going to the grave as a means to quicken us to our present work, by all which we see how much the serious remembrance of the days of darkness must needs contribute to our readiness and preparedness for these days. Therefore, be much in this work. For my own part, I have hardly found any one thing more quickening and engaging upon my spirit than this. And souls, I would beg you, as you would live forever, think often of death.

Second, would you indeed set all things right in your souls and make all ready for a dying hour? Then be not fond of long life here in this world but rather covet to live as much as possible in a little time. I would speak of each distinctly.

(1) Be not fond of long life here in this world. A fond hope and desire of long life here is one of the greatest enemies to a true preparation of soul for our departure hence. For pray observe, take a man that is fond of long life here, and all his thoughts and projects are for this world. He is wholly taken up about and carried out after the concerns of time, scarce allowing himself one serious thought for death and eternity. A sad instance you have hereof in this rich man (Luke 12:19); he reckoned upon many years, upon a long life here; and what are the things he is taken up about? Verily the things of this world only, the increase of his goods, and where to store his treasures. Fond hopes and desires of long life here will certainly produce great delays, if not utter neglects, in the great work and concern of our souls and eternity. As ever therefore you would have all right and well in the concerns of your souls when you come to die, be not fond of long life here, but sit as loose in your thoughts, hopes, and desires, both of this life and all the enjoyments of it, as possibly you can. And indeed, my beloved, to reason it a little with you, why should you be

fond of long life here? Why should you covet a long day in this world? I would only plead with you in two things as to this.

(i) What is this world, and what have we here, that we should covet a long stay? Is this world such a sweet, such an amiable, such a desirable thing? It is an angry world, a frowning world, a dirty world, a bewitching, ensnaring world. It is a vast, howling wilderness; a strange land; a house of bondage; a troublesome, tempestuous sea; an "Aceldama"—a field of blood, such as I am sure it is oftentimes to the poor saints and people of God. And what have we here? Why, here we have "fears within, and fightings without, troubles on every side," and from all hands: from friends, from enemies, from men, from devils. Here we have sorrows, snares, losses, wounds, deaths, dangers, temptations, seductions, disappointments, "vexation of spirit." And truly, little else is to be expected by us here except that which is worse than all this—namely, daily raisings and boilings of lust; violent eruptions of corruption; great aboundings of sin and iniquity, both in ourselves and others; continual breakings with God and departings from Him, renewing and increasing sin and guilt daily. Indeed, this world is full of sin and temptation to sin. It is (as Augustine speaks of it) "all temptation"; and as it is all temptation, so it is little else but sin, and why should we covet a long stay here? "Why," says one of the ancients, "should we so much desire that life, in which, by how much the longer we live, by so much the more we sin; and the more numerous our days are, the more numerous will our sins be?" Who would desire to stay long in a prison or a dungeon, in a state and place of sin and sorrow? And such is this world.

(ii) Is there not a better life, a better place, a better state for our souls to long and aspire after? What do you think of the life above: a whole eternity spent in the divine presence, in the bosom of divine love, a life of love, a life of pleasure, a life of joy, a life of admiration, a life of holiness—perfect and unspotted holiness, a life every way correspondent to the divine life and the divine will? Is not this a better life? To be with Christ is best of all (Phil. 1:23). To possess a mansion in our Father's house, prepared by our Lord and Head, Jesus Christ, for us; to live forever in the vision and fruition of Father, Son, and Spirit; to dwell in the heavenly city, where no unclean thing can enter; to join in with the glorious hosts of saints and angels above, and with them to spend a whole eternity in songs of praise and hallelujahs to God and the Lamb; to take up all our waters at the Fountainhead; and indeed to dive and bathe unchangeably in the Fountain of all delights at the Father's right hand—O how sweet is this life! And how much to be desired by us! In a word, my beloved, the saints, when in the best frame, have many of them been so far from being fond of long life here that indeed they have thought it long till the time came when they should go hence and be no more, crying out with a holy impatience, "Why is his chariot so long in coming? why tarry the wheels of his chariot?" (Judg. 5:28).

(2) Covet to live much in a little time. It is said of the reverend and worthy divine, Dr. John Preston, that he desired to, and accordingly did, live much in a little time. And our Lord Himself (you know) did not live long in this world, but He lived much in a little time; He did much work in a few days for God and souls. And indeed, it is not a long life, but a fruitful life, that is most amiable, most desirable, and most like His life, who is life itself. It is not he that lives many years, but he that lives much in a few years, that is the most happy soul. I know those whose ambition it is not to live long but to live fruitfully and to do as much as possibly they can in a little time. And might they have their opinion or choice, it would be this: to live much in a little time and then have their dismission to rest. And, my beloved, let this be your choice

and your ambition: be casting about in yourselves how you may live much in a little time, how you may compass much spiritual work and business in a few days. Labor to treasure up much grace, much experience of God and His love, to bring a large revenue of glory to Him, and the like. And for this end possess your souls with a deep sense of the exceeding worth and preciousness of time, and accordingly set yourselves to redeem it, looking upon the loss thereof to be the greatest loss in the world (Eph. 5:16).

We are commanded to redeem the time; and what is it to redeem the time but to esteem time as precious, as a thing of incomparable worth and value, and accordingly to make the best and highest improvement of it for the honor of God, and good of our souls, that possibly we can? It is to fill up our time with duty, and our duties with grace; to make use of time for those ends, for which time is given us; not to eat, and drink, and solace ourselves in the creature, but to serve and honor the Creator; "to work out our salvation"; to get acquaintance with God and Christ; to make sure of heaven and a blessed eternity. O sirs! Look upon your time as precious; so indeed it is. Time is the most weighty and momentous thing in the world. "Where the tree falleth, there it shall be" (Eccl. 11:3). As it is with us when we go out of time, so it will be with us to all eternity; and this we should be much in the thoughts of, accounting therefore the loss of time to be the greatest loss. It is a weighty saying, which I have read in one of the ancients: "It is a great and heavy loss indeed," says he, "when we neither do good, nor think good [and let me add, nor get good], but we suffer our hearts to wander abroad about vain and unprofitable things; and yet it is too difficult to restrain or keep them back from these things."

Truly, there is no loss like the loss of time: the loss of estate, the loss of trade, the loss of this or the other outward comfort is nothing to the loss of time. These being lost may be recovered again, but time being lost can never be recovered more. Accordingly set yourselves to redeem it, and do it as much as possibly you can, accounting that day lost wherein you have not done something for God and your souls. The truth is, we live no more than we are conversant in the work of God and our souls. For as for that which we call life, that is not spent in this work, it is not indeed to be accounted life.

Third, would you indeed set all things right in your souls, make all ready for a dying hour? Then think much and often with yourselves how great a change death will make with you whenever it comes. Death is a change, and in many respects the greatest change which the sons of men are to pass through. "All the days of my appointed time will I wait, till my change come" (Job 14:14). Job had many changes, and great changes. "Changes and war are against me," as he complained (Job 10:17), but no change like this of death. This was the great change, and this he waited for all his days. Indeed, death is a great change to every man and woman, come when or how it will. It is (as you have heard) that which deprives men of all their enjoyments here; which dissolves the union betwixt soul and body; which turns the body to dust and putrefaction; and (which is unspeakably more than this) it is that through which the soul enters into the immediate presence of God and states it in eternity. It is a change from time to eternity, from works to rewards, a reward suitable to the work we have here been doing, whether it be good or evil. And is not this a great change? Take a few hints in particular about it, to show the greatness of it.

(1) It is such a change as all other changes upon the outward man are but leading and introductory unto, and into which at last they all issue and resolve themselves. We pass through many changes here in this world. We may say as Job,

"changes and war are upon us." But these are but leading and preliminary, as it were, to this last and great change; these all are, or should be, to us monitors of this last change, and do but a little darkly shadow it out unto us.

(2) It is such a change as calls for great spiritual changes to pass upon us here, to fit and prepare us for it: a change in our minds, a change in our wills, a change in our affections, a change in our conversation, a change in our whole man—a real change, a thorough change, a universal change. "Old things are passed away; behold, all things are become new" (2 Cor. 5:17). The mind must be changed from darkness to light, from ignorance to knowledge in spiritual things; the will must be changed from enmity to subjection, from rebellion to obedience to God and His laws; the affections must be changed from earthliness to heavenliness, from carnality to spirituality; the conversation must be changed from sin to holiness, from vanity and looseness to strictness and seriousness in walking with God. O how great must that change be that calls for so many and so great changes to fit and prepare us for it!

(3) It is such a change, as though it do not put us out of being, yet it puts us into a quite other manner of being than ever we yet had; a change which sets us naked before the tribunal of God, to receive a definitive sentence of life or death from Him; a change which brings us into the immediate sight of God, either as a gracious Father or as a revenging Judge; a change which fully opens the eyes of the soul and makes him to see both grace and sin, heaven and hell—grace in its amiableness, sin in its odiousness, heaven in its glory, and hell in its horror. For, my beloved, whatever we are—whether good or bad, saints or sinners—yet when we die, our eyes will be fully opened to see these things. If we be good, we shall see them with joy and exultation; if we be bad, we shall see them with anguish and confusion of soul.

Fourth, it is such a change as makes us capable of, and actually put us into, unspeakably greater things, either of happiness or misery, comfort or confusion, than ever here we knew or were capable of: a change which in one moment, in the twinkling of an eye, carries the soul from small first fruits to the full vintage, from a few drops to a bottomless, boundless ocean of either happiness or vengeance, delight or torment. And withal there leaves him without any possibility of change or alteration forever but that of its reunion with the body; for it is such a change as leaves the state of the soul forever unchangeable. O then think much and often with yourselves how great a change death will make with you! Certainly did men think and consider with themselves how great a change death will make with them when it comes, they would not leave the matters of their souls in such disorder and discomposure, in such an unready posture for it as they do.

Fifth, would you indeed set all right in your souls and make all ready for a dying hour? Then presently set upon soul work, without admitting of the least delay or procrastination upon any account whatsoever: delays and procrastination in the work of our souls and eternity is the highway to death and ruin. What was it that ruined the foolish virgins but their delays in this great work and their neglect of the great concerns of their souls, till it was too late to mind them (Matt. 25:1–13)! Felix also was in a fair way, and had a fair opportunity before him, to have provided for another world; but he delayed, and his delay (for ought we know) was his ruin (Acts 24:25). Truly the heart is very apt to delay and procrastinate soul work. It is apt to cry out, "Tomorrow, tomorrow." Hence it is that the Scripture calls so often upon us for a speedy engaging in the work of our souls. The Scripture says, "Now is the accepted time; behold, now is the day of salvation" (2 Cor. 6:2) and "To day if ye will hear his voice, harden not your hearts" (Heb.

3:7–8). And if the Scripture says, "Now," why should you talk of hereafter? If the Scripture says, "To day," why should you talk of tomorrow?

Augustine confesses this, and withal tells us, there is scarce any end of delays if once we give way to them. "I delayed," says he, "to be converted to God, and put off my living to him from day to day." And elsewhere he tells us that when God called upon him to awake to his work, he returned nothing but a few sleepy words: "Anon, Lord," says he. "Anon; bear with me a little. But this anon and anon had no end, and this bear with me a little went on a long way." Take heed of this, this has been the ruin of thousands, and ten thousands. How many have been convinced that it is their duty and interest both to fall in with the work of God and their souls to make preparation for another world? But they have put it off till hereafter, and satisfied their consciences with resolutions hereafter to do so and so, and have thus lost their season. O fall presently without delay upon soul work. And to quicken you a little hereunto, consider four things.

(1) Consider the unreasonableness of delays. No just plea can be made, nor true account given, why you should delay your soul work one moment. The devil and a man's own heart will make many pleas, but no just plea can be made. They will tell you it is too soon; you are young and have time enough before you, what need you engage so soon? But is this a rational plea? Is it too soon to be saved, too soon to be happy, too soon to secure your eternal interest? Is it too soon to lay hold on eternal life? Is it too soon to know and enjoy God? Is it too soon to be out of danger of perishing eternally? Why, truly it cannot be too soon for these things; besides, God calls for your youth: "Remember now thy Creator in the days of thy youth" (Eccl. 12:1). And He greatly values "the kindness of thy youth" (Jer. 2:2). Again, they will suggest, that such and such a

business must be dispatched, such a work done and carried off your hands, and then you may attend this work. "Lord," said he to Christ, "suffer me first to go and bury my father." And said another, "Lord, I will follow thee; but let me first go bid them farewell, which are at home" (Luke 9:57–61).

But friends, let me ask you if there be any business to be dispatched like the business of your souls and eternity. Is there anything upon your hand that is of so much worth as your souls and of so much weight as eternity? Is there anything you are so nearly concerned to mind as that which is indeed the one thing necessary, even the saving of your souls? Oh! The whole world is nothing to this, and the greatest concernments on earth are but trifles to this concern. Again, they will tell you it is an inconvenient season, and hereafter the work may be better done and minded by you than now it can, which was Felix's case in the place before mentioned (Acts 24:25). But hearken, soul, are you sure of another season? And are you sure that will be a more convenient season? Surely, no. If it be not convenient today, you may fear it will be less convenient tomorrow; that devil and deceitful heart that tells you it is not convenient now will make provision that it shall be less convenient hereafter. O therefore break through all these pleas and fall speedily upon soul work.

(2) Consider the danger of delays. Delays in this case are exceedingly dangerous; one day's, yea (for anything I know), one hour's delay herein may prove your eternal undoing! It may prove the loss of Christ, the loss of heaven, the loss of your soul, and all forever. Alas! Are you sure you shall live one day, one hour more in this world? For ought you know, the next moment you could go "down to the grave" (Job 21:13). But in case you should live longer in the world, are you sure the gospel and the means of grace shall be continued to you? If you should not be taken from the world, yet the gospel may

be taken from you; though the day of your life may last a while longer, yet the day of gospel grace and mercy may suddenly expire. And if that be once gone, all the tender overtures of Christ, all the offers of grace, all the exhibitions of life and salvation are gone; if the gospel be once gone, your season is gone, and your soul is gone, and your salvation is gone, and that forever; therefore, says the apostle, "Now is the accepted time," speaking of the day of gospel mercy; "now is the day of salvation" (2 Cor. 6:2).

Or, grant that you should live and the gospel should be continued to you, as to the outward means, yet are you sure that the day and season of grace will last any longer than this present moment? Remember that sad word which the Lord breathed out with tears in His eyes over neglectful Jerusalem: "If thou hadst known, even thou, at least in this thy day, the things which belong unto thy peace! but now they are hid from thine eyes" (Luke 19:42). Alas! How soon may God withdraw His Spirit from you? How soon may He call home His grieved Spirit from your neglecting, resisting soul, once for all, saying, "My Spirit shall not always strive with man" (Gen. 6:3)? How soon may God seal you up under judicial blindness and hardness of heart, so that you shall never be able to believe or do anything for the good of your soul in order for another world? You talk of tomorrow and hereafter, but who knows but that before tomorrow God may clap the seal of a hard heart and a blind mind upon you? So as that though you should live a thousand years and withal enjoy the fairest means that ever any soul enjoyed, yet you should be never able to believe or repent, to do anything for the working out of your salvation. It is often His way of proceeding with neglecting, delaying ones (Isa. 6:10).

O how soon may the oath of God go forth against you? You talk of tomorrow; but alas! Who knows but that before tomorrow God may swear in His wrath that you shall not enter into His rest? It is what is threatened against such as will not hear His voice today but harden their hearts against Him (Heb. 3:7–11). There is a time when God's oath goes forth against souls and such and such sinners for their contempt and neglect of Christ and grace, a time not only when God says but swears, and that in wrath, that they should never enter into His rest. And if once God's oath is gone out against a man, that man is past recovery; then farewell Christ, and heaven, and soul, and all forever. O how dangerous are delays! Therefore, take heed of them and fall presently upon soul work.

(3) Consider the disadvantage of delays. Delays herein are disadvantageous as well as dangerous. Indeed, were there no danger in them (I mean as to the eternal state), yet the disadvantage of them is so great as, if rightly considered, might be enough to antidote the soul against them and engage it presently in the work which relates to another world. Pray consider it a little; by delays the soul loses much sweet communion with Christ, and many a blessed communication of love from Him, which he might enjoy. The sooner we fall upon the work of heaven and eternity, the sooner we come to a taste and beginning of heaven and a blessed eternity in our souls. O the sweet embraces, the blessed discoveries, the glorious incomes of love and delight that the soul loses by his delays to get into Christ, and to walk with God, and to mind eternal concerns!

Poor soul, by your delays you have lived upon husk and swill all your days hitherto, whereas you might have eaten bread in your Father's house and drunk wine new in your Father's kingdom. You have lived on the muddy, dungy, drossy delights of sin and the creature, whereas you might have solaced and delighted your soul with those crystal streams of undefiled pleasures, which are at Christ's and His Father's right hand. Besides, by delays the work of your soul grows more difficult; hereby corruption grows more strong and the heart grows more hard. By every day's delay, the old enmity strengthens itself and the soul is more and more settled upon its lees. For accustomedness in sinning hardens the heart in sin, as is hinted in Jeremiah 13:23. Every day the soul is more alienated from Christ and hardened against Him. At best, if your soul does at last come to see its need of Christ and desires to close with Him, and to mind the work and concerns of another world, yet the longer you delay this business, the greater temptations you will have to get over. For though now your heart says it is too soon, yet after a few days' delay it will say it is too late; it will be apt to conclude that now your day is over and now Christ will have nothing to do with you. O why should you be such an enemy to your own soul as to run it upon these disadvantages? Rather, avoid them by falling presently upon soul work.

(4) Consider the sinfulness of delays and the horrible guilt they bring upon the soul. As delays are dangerous and disadvantageous, so they are sinful too, exceeding sinful and provoking to the God of heaven. The truth is, were there no danger in them, no disadvantage by them to the soul, yet the sinfulness of them is such as should make us afraid of them. In every day's delay to mind and pursue soul work, there is positive rebellion and disobedience to the will and command of God. For the command is, "To day if ye will hear his voice, harden not your hearts" (Heb. 3:7–8). By delaying, therefore, you rebel against the commandment. In every day's delay to mind and pursue soul work, there is horrible unkindness and ingratitude to God and Christ, which surely is a black sin and brings great guilt upon the soul. God spares you time after time, when He might cast you off the next moment. And this He does that you may pursue the work of your souls and eternity; and O what unkindness, what ingratitude must it be in us to neglect and put off this work? In every delay to mind and

pursue soul work there is much contempt of Christ and grace; and this is that which makes it be exceeding sinful. Christ offers Himself and His grace to you; He offers you life, He offers you peace, He offers you pardon, He offers you righteousness, He offers you strength, He offers you all the treasures of heaven, and withal calls upon you to accept these offers and to take home these things to yourselves. But you, by your delays, pour contempt upon all; you in effect say, "Neither Christ nor His grace, neither Christ nor the purchase of His blood are worth minding, worth looking after."

O what contempt is this? And what sin is this? By delays you do in effect say there is something better than Christ and something of greater concern to you than salvation by Christ; you plainly say that indeed you will have Christ hereafter, and salvation hereafter, but for the present you had much rather have your lusts and worldly pleasures. O tremble at the thought of this, and let it frighten you out of your delays, and put them immediately upon soul work! In a word, never any pretended that they minded the concerns of their soul, union with Christ, walking with God, making sure their calling and election too soon; many have repented that they have minded these things so late.

I remember a bitter complaint of Augustine in his book of confessions: "I have loved Thee too late," said he. "O Thou so ancient, and yet so new a beauty, I have loved Thee too late." He bewails that he had so long laid out his love upon the creature and not given Christ his love. Could you ask all the saints in heaven whether ever they repented that they minded the work of Christ, and their souls, so soon, they would tell you, no, they repented of nothing but that they minded it so late.

Once more, therefore, let me call upon you to fall immediately upon soul work, and never rest till your heart cries out to God as Augustine did, when God had really showed him

Himself and made him sensible of his sins. "When God," said
he, "had showed my sins and misery, there arose a great storm
within me, which carried with it a great shower of tears; and
indeed, I let loose the reins of tears, crying out to God in such
words as these, O Lord, how long, how long wilt Thou be angry?
How long shall it be said, tomorrow, and tomorrow? Wherefore
may it not be now? Why may there not an end be put to my
sin and filthiness this very hour?" And indeed, God made that
very season the season of his conversion. So labor to see your
sin and misery so far as you may cry out with a holy restlessness
to God, "How long shall it be said, tomorrow, and tomorrow?
Why may it not be turned to Thee now? Why may not my soul
be engaged in the work of heaven and eternity now?"

Fifth, would you indeed set all right in your souls and
make all ready for a dying hour? Then be much and importunate with God in prayer to teach you so to number your
days as to apply your hearts to wisdom. This I ground upon
Psalm 90:12, where Moses, the man of God, is found in this
practice: "Lord," says he, "teach us so to number our days, that
we may apply our hearts unto wisdom." As Mollerus says, "To
number our days, is not to number them in an arithmetical,
but a spiritual way; it is not to cast up how many days the life
of man consists of, that is easily done; but it is spiritually and
practically to consider, and lay to heart, the shortness and
uncertainty of our lives, together with the various miseries
and calamities that do attend them." It is seriously and fiducially to contemplate the vanity of life as short and uncertain
and as attended with sorrows, miseries, and innumerable troubles, and to apply your heart to wisdom. It is to make religion,
and the work of a man's soul, his main business; it is to make it
his great business and endeavor to get an interest in God and
Christ in the covenant of grace and eternal life, and in time
to provide for and make sure of a blessed eternity; it is to set

a man's whole soul to the work of God and his own salvation. Now, as ever you would indeed make ready for a dying hour, beg of God to teach you thus to number your days and thus to apply your hearts to wisdom. There are two things I would observe, and so close this.

(1) That such a numbering of our days is what the best of saints need and may make great use of. Moses was a very holy man, and he looked upon it as a work useful and of great importance to him to contemplate the vanity of life and to think of the shortness and uncertainty of his abode here. The most holy souls need this; the most holy souls need humbling, they need weaning from this world, they need quickening unto duty, they need to have their hearts awakened, to mind heaven and a future life, and the right numbering of our days is that which greatly conduces thereunto.

(2) Observe that this is a work needful and useful for the best of saints to be employed in, so it is a work about their own strength and that which they need divine assistance to enable them unto. Moses was an eminently holy man, and yet he saw he had need of this, so he saw it was a work above his power, and therefore he goes to God and puts in himself among the rest and prays for His teaching herein. Let us do likewise; let us lie much at the foot of God for His teachings, whereby we may be enabled so to number our days as thus to apply our hearts unto wisdom. Beg Him to make us see the vanity and uncertainty of our lives, and that so as effectually to engage us to make out after a better life.

CHAPTER 8

Pursue Christ, Assurance, Peace, a Good Conscience, and Purity

Wherein more particular helps and directions are laid down in order to the setting of things right, and making all ready for a dying hour.

I would come nearer this great business, and give you some more particular directions, in order to your making all ready for a dying hour.

First, would you indeed have all things right in the matters of your souls for a dying hour? Then get into Christ, get union with Christ, and an interest in Christ by believing. Union with Christ and an interest in Christ is most required and necessary to fit and prepare us for a dying hour, and if we do not have it, we can have nothing set right, nothing in order, nothing in readiness for that hour. You know how the Scripture speaks: "He that hath the Son hath life; and he that hath not the Son of God hath not life" (1 John 5:12) and "There is therefore now no condemnation to them which are in Christ Jesus" (Rom. 8:1).

O my beloved, we shall live or die, be saved or damned forever according as we do or do not get a union with Christ. This is that which lies at the bottom and foundation of all—of all our hopes, of all our mercies, of all our comforts, of all our acceptation and communion with God, of all grace on earth, and all glory in heaven. And without it, whatsoever our attainments in religion are, whatever our profession may be, whatever place or esteem we may have in the church of God, though never so raised or eminent, yet we have not anything that will avail us in a dying hour. I remember a saying of a learned man, "That you may live in death," said he, "get into Christ, implant yourself into Christ by believing. Faith joins and unites us to Christ, and they that are in Christ cannot die, for Christ is their life." And indeed, if we have union with Christ, He will be life in death itself to us. "Blessed are the dead which die in the Lord"; that is, die having union with Christ, being implanted into Christ (Rev. 14:13). If we have union with Christ, He will not be only life in death to us, but He will even turn death itself into life, the King of Terrors into a King of Comforts, insomuch that the soul shall be able to triumph over it, as the apostle does (1 Cor. 15:55–57). Whereas without this, without union with Christ and an interest in Christ, we shall never be able to look death in the face with comfort, but shall, when we come to die, be some of the most miserable spectacles in the world. It is the speech of a worthy divine, who is long since gone hence, "A Christless dying man or woman," said he, "is one of the saddest spectacles in the world." For a man to be dying and not Christless, that is comfortable; for such a one dies but to live forever; he dies the death of nature, to live the life of glory. For a man to be Christless and not dying is something tolerable. Who knows but at the next meeting at an ordinance may be the time of God's love to him, of drawing him into Christ? But for a man to be dying and Christless—Christless and dying too—that is intolerable; that is terrible indeed, for such a one dies to be damned, and he is going off from all hopes and possibilities of mercy forever.

Oh, therefore above all press after union with Christ and an interest in Christ. This was Paul's great care and solicitude to the very last, that so he might go off the stage with comfort, and that for which he accounted "all things…but dung," as most base and vile (Phil. 3:8–9). O soul, did you know and consider of how much weight and importance an interest in Christ is to you with reference to your eternal happiness, you would cry out as eagerly for Christ as Rachel did for her children, saying, "Give me Christ, or else I die; give me union with Christ, and an interest in Christ, or I am undone eternally." O look to the great uniting act of faith; make a right choice of Christ; choose Him as your Lord and Head, your King and Savior; and renew your choice of Him every day, resigning up yourselves entirely to Him to be saved and governed by Him in His own way.

Second, would you indeed have all right and made ready in the matters of your souls for a dying hour? Then press after a firm and unshaken assurance of an interest in God, and His love, and of your right and title to eternal life, of another and better life than this is here. Without some good evidence for heaven and some well-grounded assurance of an interest in God and eternal life, things are not ready with us, nor are we in such a preparedness for a dying hour, as we ought to be. Though a man have an interest in God and His love, though he has a right and title to eternal life and happiness, yet as long as he is in the dark, and at an uncertainty in his own soul about it, things are out of order with him, and he is greatly unready for a dying hour. As our interest in this is required to our dying happily, so the sight and assurance of that interest is requisite to our dying comfortably.

Indeed, when a man has attained to some good evidence for heaven, to some well-grounded assurance of his interest in God and Christ, then are things in a good posture with him in reference to a dying hour; then he can triumph over death as Job did, when he could say, "I know that my redeemer liveth" (Job 19:25), and as the apostle seems to speak of it, "For we know that if our earthly house of this tabernacle were dissolved, we have a building of God, an house not made with hands, eternal in the heavens. For in this we groan, earnestly desiring to be clothed upon with our house which is from heaven" (2 Cor. 5:1–2). None of you do comfortably leave your house unless you have another to go unto; much less can you comfortably quit this world unless you have some well-grounded assurance of another and a better life. Take a man that is in the dark, and at a loss as to his interest in God and Christ, and he knows not what death will do to him, not where it will lodge him, whether in heaven or hell, whether upon the throne of glory or in the prison of eternal darkness, in the bosom of Christ's love or under the revelation of His infinite and eternal wrath. And is such a one ready for a dying hour? Surely, no. As ever, therefore, you would have things right and ready within indeed for a dying hour, you must press after an assurance of your interest in God and Christ; you must do as the apostle exhorts: "Give diligence to make your calling and election sure" (2 Peter 1:10). You must every day press after a fuller and firmer assurance as to your eternal interest. You must be much in faith, much in prayer, much in examining your evidences, much in proving your state, much in looking after the seal and evidences of the blessed Spirit, which is indeed all in all, and never rest until you can say, "My Lord, and my God, my heaven, my glory; God is the rock of my heart, and my portion forever." O then all will be sweet and well with you. This is that which the saints of old have labored after with their whole might. "Say unto my soul," says David to God, "I am thy salvation" (Ps. 35:3). "Set me as a seal upon thine heart, as a seal upon thine arm" (Song 8:6). This Augustine pressed much after. "Lord," said he, "tell me what Thou art to me. Say unto my soul, I am your salvation; so say it, that I may hear it. Behold, the ears of my heart are before Thee; open them, O Lord, and say unto my soul, I am your salvation."

O my beloved, this is worth pressing after, for this is the most welcome news a poor soul can possibly hear, to be told that God is his, and heaven is his, and eternal life is his. And when once this news is come, then welcome life and welcome death; welcome time and welcome eternity. Then the soul can say, "O sweet eternity! O blessed eternity!" O be not satisfied without some good assurance of God's love to your souls and your right and title to heaven and eternal life—yea, without the fullest assurance that is attainable here! For know that there are degrees in assurance itself. The Scripture mentions three degrees of assurance. First, there is assurance: "The work of righteousness shall be peace; and the effect of righteousness quietness and assurance for ever" (Isa. 32:17) and "Give diligence to make your calling and election sure," as in that place before quoted. Second, there is much assurance: "Our gospel came not unto you in word only, but also in power, and in the Holy Ghost, and in much assurance" (1 Thess. 1:5). Third, there is a full assurance: "We desire that every one of you do shew the same diligence to the full assurance of hope unto the end" (Heb. 6:11). Now, my beloved, I would not have you satisfied without assurance, without much assurance—yea, without a full assurance. The more full your assurance is, the more cheerfully, joyfully, and triumphantly you will die.

Third, would you indeed have all right, all in order in the matter of your souls for a dying hour? Then labor to maintain a constant actual peace with God, every day making even with Him and renewing the sense of His pardoning love in your souls as a firm union with Christ and a well-grounded assurance of an interest in God and eternal life; so also an actual peace with God, and a daily renewed pardon from Him, is requisite to a thorough readiness and preparedness for a dying hour. David had an interest in God—yea, and his interest was clear to him. Yet how solicitous was he to get all even before God and him? And how uncomfortable was it with him till he had renewed his peace with God, when by his fall it had been broken (Ps. 51:8, 12)? This also is what is evidently held forth in Job 7:21, where Job pleads thus with God: "Why dost thou not pardon my transgression, and take away my iniquity? for now shall I sleep in the dust; and thou shalt seek me in the morning, but I shall not be." In the verse before, he acknowledged he had sinned, and here he intimates that God frowned on him for his sin; the sense of pardoning love was not renewed in his soul, which here therefore he pleads for, and that upon this account, because he was speedily to die, intimating he could not die with comfort till he had a renewed sense of God's pardoning love. And this is the very thing which David begs in the psalm of my text, in order to his comfortable going hence—namely, that God would take away his transgression (Ps. 39:8).

As long as there is any sin, any guilt lying upon our consciences, any sin unpardoned, any difference between God and us, any frowns in His face toward us, we are unready for death and cannot with that comfort and boldness of spirit welcome it as we ought. But when our peace with God is maintained and we have a renewed sense of His pardoning love in our souls, then are things right and in order with us indeed, and we may think of death with boldness and comfort. And therefore mind this, as ever you would be found ready for a dying hour: every day even things between God and you; every day get a fresh sense of pardon from Him.

(1) As near as possibly may be, do nothing that may occasion any breach between God and you, or raise any frowns in

His face toward you. If you do not break with God, He will not break with you. All breaches as to peace and friendship between God and us begin on our part; yea, neither will God break with us for little things, in case they be not allowed by us, but watched and striven against; therefore, as near as possibly you can, do nothing to break and interrupt your peace with God for one moment. And because when you have done all, many things may and will fall out (we having sinful, sinning hearts and living in a world of snares and temptations) for which God may justly frown upon us.

(2) Let us every day make even with Him. In the close of every day let us consider wherein we have broken with God, come short of duty, given any grief and distastes to His Holy Spirit, and by faith and prayer let us sue out the pardon of it; and let us not lie down, if possible, without some intimation of His pardoning love. For which end,

(i) We should exercise faith in the blood and advocateship of Jesus Christ, "Whom God hath set forth to be a propitiation through faith in his blood, to declare his righteousness for the remission of sins" (Rom. 3:25). And indeed Christ has set up a standing office in heaven, which we may call the pardon office; He procures new pardons for His people daily under their new sins: "We have an advocate with the Father, Jesus Christ the righteous: and he is the propitiation for our sins" (1 John 2:1–2). Have daily recourse to the blood of Christ; truly without it there's no living. The best, the holiest on earth have daily need of His blood, and should have daily recourse unto it, for the maintaining of their peace and for the renewing of God's pardoning love in their souls.

(ii) We should be humbly and earnestly importunate with God in prayer, resolving not to let Him go without His blessing, carrying upon our spirits the sense of the worth and also of our unworthiness of it. Thus the holy men of God of old have done. They have sued out the pardon of their sins by faith and prayer, and gotten a fresh sense of God's love when they have broken with Him, as I might instance in Job, in David, and others. We should every day pray, as that father did: "O Lord," said he, "do not after the manner of a judge, weigh or consider what I have done, what I have spoken, what I have thought, but blot out all my sins with Thy own blood." And as another of them did: "Lord," said he, "there is that in me which may offend Thy holy eyes. I know and confess it, but who shall cleanse me! Oh, to whom shall I fly for relief but to Thee? O hide not Thy face from me." Truly, when we have walked most watchfully, most circumspectly, many things may and will fall out that may offend the pure eyes of God's glory, which we should confess and bewail before Him, suing out the pardon of them by the blood of His Son. Some of the saints have made this their daily practice and so have maintained their peace for many years together; and when they have come to die they gloriously triumphed over death and have gone off the stage with much comfort, and so should we.

Fourth, would you indeed have all right? All in order in your souls for a dying hour? Then be true and faithful to your own consciences, that you may have them for you, and not against you, both while you live and when you die. Conscience, my beloved, is Christ's deputy or vice-regent in the soul. It is both a judge and a witness for God within us; it either accuses or excuses, acquits or condemns (Rom. 2:15). And according as conscience is either for us or against us, so we are either ready or not ready, prepared or not prepared for death and judgment. If we have the witness and judgment of our consciences for us, then have we boldness and comfort both in life and in death; then we can welcome death's approach to us. But if the witness and judgment of conscience be against us, then death cannot but be terrible to us. "Our rejoicing is this," says the apostle, "the testimony of our conscience, that in simplicity and godly sincerity, not with fleshly wisdom, but by the grace of God, we have had our conversation in the world" (2 Cor. 1:12). And again, "If our heart condemn us, God is greater than our heart, and knoweth all things. Beloved, if our heart condemn us not, then have we confidence toward God" (1 John 3:20–21).

Oh my beloved, like peace with God, so a sound and holy peace with a man's own conscience (that is to say, to have the witness and judgment of a man's own conscience for him and not against him) is highly requisite for a right disposing and preparing of us for a dying hour. As ever, therefore, you would have all ready and in order against such an hour, mind this, and look after this: be sure you carry it so to your own consciences as that you may have them always for you, and not against you, while you live, and for you, and not against you, when you come to die. In order to which, mind these two things.

(1) Labor to get your consciences well enlightened and informed, and be much with God in prayer in order thereto beg and implore God for a true and faithful conscience, a conscience that will bear a true and faithful witness in your souls and that will pass a right judgment upon things, both upon your state and actions. In Hebrews 10:22 we read of a true heart, or a true conscience—that is, a conscience rightly informed, a conscience that bears a true and faithful witness, that passes a true and faithful judgment upon things. Such a conscience should we beg of God and labor by all means possible to attain unto. Oh, my beloved! It is a dangerous thing to have an erroneous conscience, a mistaking conscience, a conscience not rightly informed. For note that this is what leaves a man under a necessity of sinning, and so of grieving the Spirit of God, on the one hand, and it endangereth his peace and comforts, on the other hand. For having an erroneous conscience, whether we obey it or obey it not, we sin;

if we obey it, we sin, because conscience commands what is not agreeable to the Word of God; if we obey it not, we sin, because we rebel against the light and dictates of conscience, omitting that which conscience tells us is a duty, though it be not a duty, or do that which conscience tells us is a sin, though it be not a sin. Labor, therefore, to get your conscience well informed and enlightened.

(2) Be sure you do nothing against the light and dictates of conscience, being rightly informed, but obey it in all things. In Job 24:13, we read of some "that rebel against the light"—that is, that do sin against their own consciences, which is double sin, a sin clothed with great aggravations and greatly unsettles us for a dying hour. But we must take heed of this and listen to the voice of conscience—conscience regulated by the Word of God. God speaks to us by our consciences, He speaks to us through His Word by our consciences, and He speaks to us through His providence by our consciences, and we should take heed of violating the dictates or speaking of conscience in the least. Does not conscience many times tell us such and such ways which we walk in are not good, and must be turned from, or we are undone forever? And now we should be true and faithful to our own consciences, and speedily turn from those ways; we should have nothing to do with anything that conscience condemns us in and for. Again, does not conscience many times tell you that such and such duties are totally neglected, or else seldom or slightly performed by you, which yet you ought to be conversant and diligent in the performance of? Now you should herein also be faithful and true to your own conscience, living up to the constant, diligent, spiritual performance of those duties. Again, does not conscience many times tell you that things are not right with you? That it is an evil frame of spirit you live in? That you are too carnal, too light, too vain, too frothy, too eager

in your pursuits of this world, and too remiss in your pursuits of heaven and eternity? Now as ever you would be ready for a dying hour, you should be faithful to your own conscience, setting that right which is amiss and hastening out of that evil frame into the contrary gracious frame.

O my beloved, if you be true and faithful to conscience, conscience will be true and faithful to you, witnessing for you, and not against you, both while you live and when you die. In a word, in all things labor to keep a good conscience; this was Paul's great care and exercise: "Herein do I exercise myself, to have always a conscience void to offence toward God, and toward men" (Acts 24:16). O this will be a sweet and blessed exercise, and the more we are found in it while we live, the more comfort will it afford us when we come to die.

Fifth, would you indeed have all things right and in order in the matters of your souls when a dying hour comes? Then labor for much purity of heart and life, and by no means admit of any sin, any corruption whatsoever; the more pure and holy we are, the more ready we are, and the better posture things are with us for a dying hour. Without holiness, says the apostle, "no man shall see the Lord" (Heb. 12:14). Holiness is necessary unto happiness; holiness is the way unto happiness; holiness is what fits and prepares us for happiness and brings unto happiness. Yea, holiness is a part of our happiness; a great part of the happiness of heaven itself lies in holiness. Accordingly, the more holy we are, the more we are suited to and prepared for the future happiness, and so for death and judgment. For that which prepares us for the future happiness, that also prepares us for death, which is but an inlet into that happiness forever.

Therefore, if you would have all things right, all things ready indeed for a dying hour, then labor for the exactest purity and holiness you can. This is that which the apostle aims at, and prays for, on the behalf of the Thessalonians, as most conducing to the preparing of them for their latter end: "And the Lord make you to increase and abound in love one toward another, and toward all men, even as we do toward you: to the end he may stablish your hearts unblameable in holiness before God, even our Father, at the coming of our Lord Jesus Christ with all his saints" (1 Thess. 3:12–13). The posture he would have them be in at the coming of Christ is the posture of unblameable holiness, which indeed is the best and readiest posture. The same things he prays for, in order to the same end, in 1 Thessalonians 5:23: "And the very God of peace sanctify you wholly; and I pray God your whole spirit and soul and body be preserved blameless unto the coming of our Lord Jesus Christ." This is that also which that other apostle enjoins in order thereunto: "Be diligent that ye may be found of him in peace, without spot, and blameless" (2 Peter 3:14). The more spotless and blameless we are in our spirits and ways, the more ready we are for death and judgment.

Oh, press after an eminency in holiness, admitting of none, no, not the least taint or tincture of sin, or sinful defilement upon any terms whatsoever! Unholy souls are unready souls; they are unready for death, unready for judgment, unready for the future life. And for men to talk of being ready for these, and yet be unholy, is the greatest folly in the world. Therefore, labor for much purity and holiness.

(1) Labor for much purity and holiness in your lives and walkings. This is what God indispensably calls for: "As he which hath called you is holy, so be ye holy in all manner of conversation; because it is written, Be ye holy; for I am holy" (1 Peter 1:15–16). We should press after universal holiness. There should be a vein and a tincture of holiness running through all we do, even our civil as well as our religious actions; we should as near as possible be dedicated and devoted to God, and our lives should be lives of walking with Him. They and

they only, who walk with God while they live, are those who will be found ready to live with God when they come to die.

As for all careless, licentious ones, let them never talk of being ready for death and the future life, for they are at an utter distance from any such thing. Indeed, ready they are, but for what? Ready for hell, ready for the wrath of God, ready for destruction. But they are not at all ready for a blessed eternity. The apostle weeps over such as being indeed thus ready: "Many walk, of whom I have told you often, and now tell you even weeping, that they are the enemies of the cross of Christ: whose end is destruction, whose God is their belly, and whose glory is in their shame, who mind earthly things" (Phil. 3:18–19). Many there are who profess and hope well of themselves, as to another life, who yet are loose and carnal, wicked and licentious in their lives and walking. They do not watch and keep their garments, but wallow in the mire of their lusts and pollutions. They stain their profession with foul, gross, and scandalous sins; at least they live and allow themselves in some secret way and haunt of sinning, indulging this and the other lust. But, my beloved, these are far indeed from being ready for a dying hour, and must expect to be cast off from God and Christ forever.

Such were those in Matthew 7:22–23: they came and cried, "Lord, Lord." They came with their gifts, parts, and privileges, but Christ sent them away with a "depart from me, ye that work iniquity." So in the beginning of Jeremiah 7, we read of some that made profession of God and His ways, and yet walked in sin and wallowed in all manner of abomination. And what is the issue? Says God, "I will cast you out of my sight" (v. 15). God will at last cast off all loose, licentious walkers. In Psalm 26:9, David prays thus: "Gather not my soul with sinners." And truly, if you would not be gathered with sinners at last, you must not walk in sin with sinners now. And as for the saints themselves, so far as they let down their watch and neglect their walking with God; so far as they give way to a loose, vain, heedless way of living; so far they have things out of order with them, and they are unready for a dying hour. "Behold I come as a thief," says Christ. "Blessed is he that watcheth, and keepeth his garments, lest he walk naked, and they see his shame" (Rev. 16:15). So far as the saints carry it unbecoming their high and holy profession (which is too frequent with them), so far they are short of that complete readiness for death and eternity they should press after.

(2) Labor for much purity and holiness in your hearts and affections. We must be pure and holy within as well as without, in our hearts and affections as well as in our lives and walking, if we would have all right indeed for a dying hour. "Who shall ascend into the hill of the LORD? or who shall stand in his holy place?" The answer is "he that hath clean hands, and a pure heart" (Ps. 24:3–4). And Christ expressly tells us, "Blessed are the pure in heart: for they shall see God" (Matt. 5:8). Indeed, impure hearts are unfit to see God, nor may impure-hearted ones expect that blessed sight. I remember a saying which I have read in one of the ancients (which I look upon to be a great saying): "Woe and alas! O Lord," said he, "how preposterous is it? How rash and unadvised? How inordinate? How remote from the rule of the Word of Thy truth and wisdom, for a man to desire to see God with an unclean heart?" O have a watchful eye upon your hearts and labor to keep them as free from any taint and tincture of sin as possibly you can.

(i) Be sure you suffer no lust to get up into the throne, where it is too often found. When sin is consented to by the will, the lust is on the throne in the heart; and indeed it is remarkable to think how soon one or another corruption will mount up into the throne in the soul if we let down our watch but a little. But oh, take heed of this, so far as any one lust whatsoever is predominant within us, so far we are marvelously unready for a dying hour. And not only so, but,

(ii) Watch narrowly against the very first risings and motions of sin within; nip lust, if possible, in the very bud and blossom. It is true, this calls upon us to have a very curious eye upon our hearts; and indeed, such an eye we should have upon them, we must have upon them, if we mean to be Christians indeed. Grace will teach a man not only to oppose the acts of sin, and to watch against the reign of any heart lust, but also to oppose the very first motions and risings of sin in the soul. And the more you do this, the better posture you are in for a dying hour.

CHAPTER 9

Pursue Deeper Levels of Grace

A further direction in order to a complete preparation for death, to press after the noblest strains of grace. Several of these pointed at, and insisted on, as tending thereunto.

Sixth, would you indeed have all ready and in order in your souls for a dying hour? Then rest not in low and ordinary, but aspire after the highest and noblest strains of grace. To better understand this, you must know that there are some higher and more noble strains of grace than ordinary, strains of grace that carry a peculiar glory and excellency in them and do in an eminent manner delight the heart of God. Indeed, every strain of grace, even the least and lowest, has a beauty and glory in it and is a pleasure to God's heart: the least dram of godly sorrow, the least holy awe of God and trembling at His Word, the least breathing of love and desire toward Him, the least leaning upon Him in a way of hope and dependence. Oh, it has a great glory in it and is a delight to God's soul: "The LORD taketh pleasure in them that fear him, in those that hope in his mercy" (Ps. 147:11).

But, my beloved, there are some more choice and eminent strains and actings of grace that are above the ordinary rate and do peculiarly delight the heart of God and bring honor

to Him; and the more you come up to these, and live under
the power of these, the more ready posture you are in for a
dying hour. Grace is the beginning of glory. It is (as a worthy
divine expresses it) "the infancy of heaven and glory"; and the
higher it rises in us, the nearer it comes to glory, and the more
it fits us for it. Therefore, I say, rest not in low and ordinary,
but covet and press after the highest and noblest strains of
grace, some of which I shall here set down, and insist a little
upon, in order to this great end of being found under the
most precise readiness for a dying hour. The noblest strains of
grace I would have you come up unto are these.

(1) For a man to be high and yet low—high in worth and
attainments but low in spirit; low in his own thoughts and
apprehensions of himself; to be humble under high and great
acquirements—this is noble grace. It is said of Athanasius
that he was "high in worth, but low in spirit." He had great
attainments but was very humble and lowly under all, which is
mentioned as a peculiar excellency in him. And I remember
a saying which I have read in one of the ancients, speaking of
humility: "For a man to be humble," says he, "in a low, despicable, abject condition; this is no great matter, but honorable
humility"—that is to say, for a man to be humble in a high and
prosperous condition, to be humble under eminent employ-
ments. This is a great thing, a rare virtue indeed.

Oh, for a man to be high in attainments, high in gifts, high
in grace, high in comforts, high in services, high in successes,
high in place and esteem among men, and yet at the same
time to be low in mind, low in heart, low in his esteem and
apprehension of himself: this is a high and eminent strain of
grace! This Paul excelled in, and it was his crown and glory;
he was a man of as high attainments and accomplishments
as most that ever lived. He was high in gifts, high in graces,
high in comforts, high in services, high in successes, high in

all true worth and excellency, and yet how low, how humble in spirit was he? How little in his own eyes and how vile in his own esteem? You know how he speaks of himself: the chief of sinners (1 Tim. 1:15); "Less than the least of all saints" (Eph. 3:8); "I am the least of the apostles, that am not meet to be called an apostle" (1 Cor. 15:9); I am nothing (2 Cor. 12:11). This also was a part of Christ's crown and glory. Who ever so eminent in gifts and graces? Who ever abounded with such glorious endowments as He? And yet who was so meek, so humble, so lowly as He? "Learn of me," says He, "for I am meek and lowly in heart" (Matt. 11:29). Two verses before, He had told us that all things were delivered unto him by the Father, and yet here He says, "I am meek and lowly in heart." He was humble under all His advancements and attainments. Oh, labor to be like Him herein; whatever your attainments are, labor to be humble under them, and that because He was so. "Blush, O dust, and ashes! Blush to think of being proud; be ashamed to be proud. God humbles Himself, and do you exalt yourself?" So one speaks. And again elsewhere, "It is intolerable impudence," says he, "that when majesty empties and humbles Himself, a vile worm should swell, and be blown up with pride."

Oh, be humble, whatever your attainments are. The more humble you are, the more precious you are in God's sight, for "hath he respect unto the lowly: but the proud he knoweth afar off" (Ps. 138:6). Yea, "God resisteth the proud" (James 4:6). "Arrogate nothing to yourself of those things that are in you but your sins; by so much the more precious you are in God's eyes, by how much the more vile and despicable you are in your own eyes," says Bernard. And to say no more, none are more ready to die than the humble and lowly person, none more unready than the proud and high minded.

(2) For a man to be full and yet empty; full of enjoyments and yet empty of the love of the world; for a man to enjoy an affluence of this world's good, a fullness of all creature comforts and contentment, and yet to be dead to all, and set loose from all, placing his whole happiness in God and Christ: this is a choice—a noble and excellent strain of grace indeed. We read of some, and but of some, in Scripture, who under an affluence of outward enjoyments have been weaned from all, and sat loose from all, and have kept up their communion with God, placing the whole rest and happiness of their souls therein; some such (I say) we read of in Scripture, but truly they are but very few, and indeed it is both a rare and difficult thing for a soul thus to do. These things especially, when enjoyed in the fullness of them, are so apt to engross the heart to themselves and to alienate it from God, and from communion with God, that it is indeed a very rare and difficult thing for a man under an affluence of them to sit loose from them and make God, and communion with God, all in all to him. It is a great saying which I have read of a learned man, "Although adversity breaks many, yet prosperity and fulness of enjoyments kills many more. And how rare a man is who in prosperity does not, at least a little in some degree or other, let down his watch, and remit his strictness and exactness in walking?" David was a wise man, and Solomon was wiser, and yet both the one and the other discovered great sin and folly through abounding prosperity. So that I say, it is both a rare and difficult thing; but by how much the more rare and difficult it is, by so much the more excellent and eminent when attained.

Oh, for a man to swim chin-deep in the streams of creature comforts and yet not so forsake the fountain of living waters, for a man to have the streams run pleasantly on each hand of him and yet to bathe and delight only in the fountain as his rest and happiness, for a man in the height of prosperity to be able to say to God, as the psalmist in his affliction did, "Whom have I in heaven but thee? and there is none upon earth that I desire beside thee" (Ps. 73:25)—this is noble grace indeed! Oh, labor to come up to this, whatever your worldly enjoyments are, though never so great, so high, so pleasant; yet as ever you would be ready for a dying hour, sit loose from all, die to all. The more dead we are to the world, the more ready we are to go out of the world. A worldly spirit, a spirit in love with this world, is most unready for a dying hour. How can he be ready to leave the world that is in love with the world? A worldly spirit is most odious to the Spirit of God and most unfruitful to the future life, and one living in that spirit cannot be fit to die. It is a great saying I have read in one: "He is perfect whose soul is alienated from the world; but," says he, "that soul is far from God to whom this miserable life is sweet"—that is to say, who is fond of these poor things here. Oh! Die daily to the world, under all your enjoyments of it, if you would indeed be ready to die.

(3) For a man to be empty and yet full; to be destitute of all outward comforts and enjoyments and yet to want nothing, but to be content, and to see all in God, and enjoy all in God; for a man to be afflicted and distressed and yet at the same time see a fullness and sufficiency of all good and happiness in a naked God, and naked godliness, and accordingly to live up unto Him and rest satisfied in Him: this is a noble strain of grace indeed. This the prophet, and in him the church, resolved upon: "Although the fig tree shall not blossom, neither shall fruit be in the vines; the labour of the olive shall fail, and the fields shall yield no meat; the flock shall be cut off from the fold, and there shall be no herd in the stalls" (Hab. 3:17). Here you see is a most sad supposition, a most forlorn and destitute condition supposed to come. Well, and what then? In case all this come to pass, what will the church do then? That the

eighteenth verse tells us: "Yet I will rejoice in the LORD, I will joy in the God of my salvation." She is resolved to live upon God, and delight herself with God; she sees enough in Him alone and sets Him and her interest in Him over against all wants, losses, and afflictions. So were the apostles in 2 Corinthians 6:10, who were "as having nothing, and yet possessing all things." They saw all in Christ and enjoyed all in Christ. "Here," as one glosses upon the place, "we possess nothing but do wander up and down from place to place; yet possessing Christ, in him we possess all things." Oh! For a man to see and enjoy all in Christ when the world frowns upon him and is low with him: this is a noble strain of grace. And let me say this, that it is an argument that we have carnal hearts if we see not all in God, and enough in God, to satisfy us and make us happy, whether we have anything or nothing of this world. Heaven, which death sends us to, if we are indeed ready for it, is nothing else but the vision and fruition of God, for there He is all in all. And certainly, if we do not see all in God now, and enough in God now, we cannot suppose ourselves to be so fully ready for death and eternity as we ought to be.

(4) For a man to have no affliction and yet to be deeply afflicted, to be wholly free from all personal affliction and yet greatly to lay to heart and be afflicted for the afflictions of God's name and people: this is glorious grace, grace in luster. It is the observation of a worthy divine that in the day of the church's trouble and affliction, when both His name and people do greatly suffer, God does sometimes leave some of His people an affluence of all outward good things. When others are stripped of all their comforts, they are full; when others are in straits, they abound; neither is there any cloud upon their tabernacle. And this God does to try them, whether they will take up in their enjoyments and forget the afflictions of His name and people. And truly not to do so, but in such

a case to lay the church's afflictions to heart and to bleed and mourn with the bleeding interest of God's name and people: this is pure grace and marvelously pleasing to God. Such grace some of the saints have come up unto.

Such graces were found in David: "And it came to pass, when the king sat in his house, and the LORD had given him rest round about from all his enemies; that the king said unto Nathan the prophet, See now, I dwell in an house of cedar, but the ark of God dwelleth within curtains" (2 Sam. 7:1–2). Mark, all was well with David; he had rest, and he dwelt in a house of cedar. He had all things suitable for and becoming a king. Ah, but all was not well with the house of God and His worship. David's house and interest prospered, but it fared not so well with the house and interest of God, and therefore all his enjoyments were as nothing to him, he so laid the sufferings of God's name and worship to heart.

The like was found in Nehemiah 2; all things were well with him in his own person. He was the king's cupbearer, and lived under the enjoyment of an affluence of all outward contentment, and yet was in deep affliction of spirit upon the account of the church's affliction. "When I heard these words," says he in chapter 1:4. These words! What words? Why, that the "remnant that are left of the captivity there in the province are in great affliction and reproach: the wall of Jerusalem also is broken down, and the gates thereof are burned with fire." So verse 4: "And it came to pass, when I heard these words, that I sat down and wept, and mourned certain days, and fasted, and prayed before the God of heaven"; and in chapter 2:1, his countenance, it is said, was "sad" upon this account. Oh, this was rare grace, choice grace! No personal affliction, yet deeply afflicted in and with the afflictions of the church: so deeply afflicted that all his personal comforts, though great, were nothing to him. The like you find in Daniel 10:2–3.

O labor to come up to this strain of grace! It may be things are well with you, and you have all that heart can wish; but if they are not so with the interest of God's name and people, you should be deeply afflicted for this in the midst of all personal comforts; and the more this spirit is in you, the more excellent your grace is.

(5) For a man to submit cheerfully to, and acquiesce in, the will of God when most sharp and severe upon this outward interest, this is a noble strain of grace. When God shall exercise a man with rending, tearing dispensations, adding sorrow to sorrow to him, breaking him with breach upon breach, causing all his waves and his billows to go over him, and yet then for him quietly to acquiesce in, and cheerfully to submit to, what God does, this is choice grace. Such grace was found in Aaron (Lev. 10:3). God slew two of his sons at once, and the dispensation was attended with so many aggravating circumstances as made it almost unparalleled, not to be equaled, so terrible was it; and yet under that great stroke, Aaron "held his peace"; he submitted freely and acquiesced cheerfully. The like was found in Job; when God had broken him all to pieces, he worships Him and blesses His name (Job 1:21–22). And this was eminent in Christ Himself and was indeed His crown and glory: "Father,... not as I will, but as thou wilt" (Matt. 26:39). He freely submits His will to the Father's, though He saw the Father coming forth against Him in a most terrible dispensation. Oh, for a poor soul to lie down at the foot of God and to be so melted into His will as cheerfully to bow to it and acquiesce in it under the sharpest dispensations; this is noble grace indeed. Oh, press after this; this is very necessary to prepare us for a dying hour, and the more of this, the more ready for that hour.

(6) For a man to maintain the acting of his faith in God, and to think honorably of Him when yet He frowns and all things seem to make against the soul: this is a noble strain

of grace. Such grace was found in Abraham, who, it is said, "against hope believed in hope…but was strong in faith" (Rom. 4:18–20). When he had no encouragement—yea, when all things opposed him—yet then he maintained his faith in God. So Job 13:15: "Though he slay me, yet will I trust in him." Oh, to love a smiting God and to trust in a slaying God; this is noble grace. For a man to maintain the acting of his faith in God when He comes forth as an enemy against him. This God calls for. He expects that when we walk in darkness and see no light, then we should trust in the name of the Lord, and so to do is noble grace (Isa. 50:10–11).

Truly it is oftentimes the case of God's people that they walk in darkness and see no light; all things seem to be against them. Possibly God frowns and afflicts; He frowns within and afflicts without. Yea, the poor soul sees nothing but difficulties and discouragements, look which way he will. He looks into his own heart, and there he cannot find any one grace or gracious dispensation; he looks into the Word, and there perhaps he cannot see any one promise that he dare lay hold upon; he looks back for former experiences, and they are all out of sight; he runs to his evidences, and they are all blotted that he cannot read. Thus he is beset with difficulties, and all things seem to make against him both within and without; and yet now, when thus in the dark, for the soul to believe in God and think well and honorably of Him, this is noble grace indeed. This is faith in luster, to call Christ Lord when He calls us a dog, and to fasten by faith upon Him when He is beating us off, as to sense at least, as it was with the Canaanitish woman (Matt. 15:26–28). This is glorious grace: for a man to think well, and hope well, and believe well in the face of frowns and discouragements. For a man when God is frowning, and smiting, cordially to say, "This is but for a time; He will smile again; He is but behind the curtain and will appear again; His desire is not to ruin me, but refine me; He is but making me to prize His grace and presence more; there is love in all this." O for a man to believe that there is love in God's heart when he sees nothing but frowns on His face and meets with nothing hardly but blows from His hand; for a man to believe that God intends nothing but good when He inflicts a variety of evils, surely this is glorious grace.

Oh, that you would labor for such grace! Such grace will look death in the face with boldness. It is a great speech which holy Rutherford has: "I lay inhibitions on my thoughts," says he, "that they receive no slander of my only beloved. Let him even say out of his own mouth, 'There is no hope; yet I will die in that sweet beguile.' Is it not so? But I shall see the salvation of God; it is my joy to believe under the water, and to die with faith in my hand, grasping Christ. Beg such grace of God."

(7) For a man to see a beauty and excellency in service as well as in enjoyment, in work as well as in reward, and accordingly to have his heart lie in it: this also is noble grace. There is a beauty and excellency in service; for a man to be used and employed for God, and to act for Him in the world, is the highest honor and excellency (next to union and communion with Him) that can be put upon a poor creature. It was the honor of Christ; it is the honor of angels. Service is better than enjoyment: "It is more blessed to give than to receive" (Acts 20:35). Now when a soul has answerable thoughts and apprehensions about it, does practically and indeed see a beauty and excellency in service for God, and accordingly is active for Him, willing to be employed by Him, and that though he has no reward at present from Him, this is noble grace.

This was found in Paul: "Unto me," says he, "is this grace given, that I should preach among the Gentiles the unsearchable riches of Christ" (Eph. 3:8). He looked on it as an honor, a favor to be employed in the work and service of Christ. And again, "I thank Christ Jesus our Lord, who hath enabled me, for that he counted me faithful, putting me into the ministry" (1 Tim. 1:12). Here he blesses Christ, his Lord and Master, for using him in His work; yea, such a worth, beauty, and excellency did he see in His service that he was content to stay out of heaven and the bosom of Christ's love, where yet he earnestly longed to be, that he might do further service for Christ in this world (Phil. 1:21–23). Oh, for a soul to long, and long earnestly, for heaven and the immediate enjoyment of Christ there, and yet to be content to stay here in a sinful, sinning, troublesome world, merely to do some further service for Christ and to honor Him yet in the discharge of His work and warfare, this is high grace.

This holy Rutherford had attained unto this; he could under high assurances of heaven be content to stay many years out of it to preach Christ. The same mind dwelt in Christ Himself, "Who went about doing good, making it his meat and drink to do his Father's will, and to finish his work." Oh! When a soul comes to this, then he is fit to live and fit to die, when with that ancient father we come to say indeed, "What is it to live, and not to live for use and service?" When we value life and days in this world no further than we are some way serviceable to Christ, this is growing grace.

(8) For a man to rejoice in the gifts, graces, and uses of others, and that though they outshine and eclipse his; for a man to rejoice to see grace flourishing in others and to see the work of God carried on by others, though he himself be laid aside and does not share in the honor of it: this is pure grace, grace in luster. Such grace was found in Moses. "Enviest thou for my sake?" said he to Joshua, who would have had him to forbid Eldad and Medad go prophesy in the camp. "Would God that all the Lord's people were prophets, and that the Lord would put his spirit upon them!" (Num. 11:29). He was

so far from envying at them that he wishes there were more of them.

Such grace was found also in John the Baptist (John 3:26–30). He rejoiced in Christ's being owned, and honored, and flocked unto, and in the increase of His esteem with men, though to his own abasement. In verse 26, some of John's disciples come and tell him that "all men come to [Christ]"; well, says he, it is but His due. "A man can receive nothing, except it be given him from heaven. Ye yourselves bear me witness, that I said, I am not the Christ.... This my joy therefore is fulfilled. He must increase, but I must decrease" (vv. 27–30). As if he had said, "It is so far from being a trouble to me that it is indeed the completing of my joy."

Such grace was found in Paul, who rejoiced that Christ was preached, though with a design to cloud and eclipse him: "Christ is preached; and I therein do rejoice, yea, and will rejoice" (Phil. 1:18). Some are apt to think, "It will be an affliction to me," says he, "that Christ is preached by any but myself; whereas indeed this is ground of great joy to me; I rejoice that though I cannot be permitted to preach Christ myself, yet that so many others do preach Him."

I remember a great speech of Luther (arguing the same grace to be in him), writing to Melanchthon, to comfort him under the opposition the work and cause of God met with in his time; the cause of God was opposed, and his work obstructed, in the sense of which Melanchthon was greatly troubled and dejected, and Luther, understanding it, writes an epistle to him to comfort and encourage him, in which he has this saying: "God," says he, "is able to raise the dead, and he is able to support his falling cause, and to raise it when fallen. If he shall not account us worthy to be used therein, let him do it by others, and make use of others." Notice he was content that the work of God should be done by others.

There are two things which I look upon to carry as pure and noble grace in them as any whatsoever. One is to be willing to be used in God's work without being taken notice of or having the honor of it. The other is for a man to rejoice to see the work of God carried on by others, though he himself be laid aside and has not the honor of being used therein. Oh, labor for such grace! Grace that will rejoice in the gifts, graces, uses, and successes of others, though you thereby are outshone.

(9) For a man to have great affliction to the name and honor of God and Christ, and to think nothing too much to do, too hard to suffer, or too dear to part with for the service and advancement thereof: this is noble grace. When a man has high and paramount affections for the name of God and Christ—loving and preferring it infinitely before all his own interests and concerns, being ready to be, do, or suffer anything for the service of it—oh, what grace is this!

Such grace some of the saints have attained unto. "Yet now," says Moses concerning Israel, "if thou wilt forgive their sin—; and if not, blot me, I pray thee, out of thy book which thou hast written" (Ex. 32:32). What is here meant by the book which God has written, I shall not now stop to inquire or determine; but to be content to be blotted out of it was, to be sure, a great act of self-denial. And this Moses desired, you see, rather than that the people should be utterly destroyed, and all because he knew how much the glory of God was concerned and would suffer by their destruction, as appears by comparing this verse with verse 12. The sum (as one observes) is that Moses prefers the glory of God before his own salvation, whose glory was conjoined with Israel's preservation in respect of the promises made to the fathers and in respect of the blasphemies which the Egyptians and other adversaries were ready to belch out against God, should He destroy them. Such grace was found also in John the Baptist in the place lately mentioned (John

3:27–30), who was content Christ should raise Himself out of His abasement. Such grace was found in Christ, who preferred His Father's glory before His own life (John 12:17, 28). Such grace was found in Paul, who was "ready not to be bound only, but also to die at Jerusalem for the name of the Lord Jesus" (Acts 21:13), for the name, the honor of Christ. Christ's honor was so dear to him that he could be content to die to serve it; he preferred it before his life.

Oh, my beloved, when a soul shall be so swallowed up with love and zeal for the glory of God and the interest of Christ in the world as that his own interests are in a manner overlooked and forgotten by him; when to see the name of God exalted shall be a man's greatest triumph and to see it debased shall be his greatest trouble; when his practical language shall be such as this—"Father, here I am; which way soever Thy glory lies, I am ready to serve Thee in it; it is happiness enough for me to glorify God; and therefore let God do with me, and let Him call me to do, whatever He will in order thereunto. Let Him, if He pleases, eclipse my name and throw my glory in the dust, so be it He will thereby raise His own name and brighten His own glory. Let Him, if He pleases, make me a footstool, and let me be trampled upon. So be it He will advance Himself into the throne thereby; let me die, if His will be so, that His glory may live. Whatever becomes of me, though I should be stripped of all, though my name and interest should rot, yet let God be magnified. Let God have honor in the world, and let the interest and kingdom of Christ prosper; it is enough, I am satisfied"—when, I say, it is thus with a soul, this speaks noble grace indeed. Oh, press after such grace! The more you love the name of God and Christ, the fitter you are either to live or to die.

(10) For a man not only to be willing to suffer but also to rejoice in suffering for the sake of Christ and the gospel, for

a man cheerfully to take up the cross of Christ and to look upon it as his crown and glory, as an honor and preferment to him: this is also a high strain of grace and is greatly pleasing to God. The cross, my beloved, in itself, "is a black, sour crab tree" (as one calls it), but though such in itself, yet as it is born for the sake of Christ, and so His cross, it is an honor, and not a reproach, a crown of glory, a royal diadem upon the head of a poor creature. "Unto you it is given in the behalf of Christ, not only to believe on him, but also to suffer for his sake" (Phil. 1:29).

Sufferings for Christ are noble, royal, honorable gifts, more honorable than the crowns and kingdoms of this world. A prison for Christ is more honorable than the most stately palaces of the greatest princes; bonds for Christ are more honorable than ropes of pearl and diamonds. Now when a soul shall look on these things as such, and accordingly rejoice in them, this is noble grace indeed; such grace was found in the disciples, who rejoiced, or, as the word is, leapt for joy, "that they were counted worthy to suffer shame for his name" (Acts 5:41), or, as the words may be rendered, that they were honored to be dishonored for Christ. So the apostle and his brethren (Rom. 5:3). "I take pleasure in infirmities," says Paul, "in reproaches, in necessities, in persecutions, in distresses for Christ's sake" (2 Cor. 12:10). So those worthies who "took joyfully the spoiling of [their] goods" (Heb. 10:34). This Christ calls us to: "Rejoice, and be exceeding glad" when men persecute you for His sake (Matt. 5:12). And again, "Count it all joy when ye fall into divers temptations" (James 1:2).

It is admirable to think how some of the saints, both in former and latter times, have gloried in the cross of Christ and even longed for it. Luther longed for the honor of martyrdom, and was ready even to envy those who were called unto it when he was not, for writing to some of his acquaintance in bonds for Christ and the gospel, he breaks out into this complaint: "O miserable me, who have been first in teaching these things, but last, and perhaps never worthy, to be a partaker of your bonds and fires." Oh, labor for such grace! We think it much if we be content to suffer, but we should rejoice in sufferings, glory in the cross, carry ourselves under sufferings for Christ, as looking upon Him to be (for so indeed they are) an honor and privilege unto us.

(11) For a man in a prosperous condition, all things going smoothly with him in the world, to be willing to loose anchor and be gone hence to heaven—yea, for a man to long, and long earnestly, for a dissolution, that he might be with Christ fully and forever with Him—this is noble grace. Take a man whose mountain of prosperity stands strong; whose paths are, as it were, strewn with roses, the roses of creature contentment; who has all that heart can wish of this world's good, the streams running pleasantly on each side of him; for such a one in such a condition to long, and long earnestly, to be gone to his dear Lord, that so he may be fully like Him, and may see Him as He is, that he may be eternally in His presence, swallowed up in the love, praises, and admiration of Him, be a perfect partaker of His life and image: this is great and glorious grace. When though a man's condition in the world be every way such as that he may well say, "It is good to be here," yet the daily pulse of his soul is that of the spouse, "Make haste, my beloved, and be thou like to a roe or to a young hart upon the mountains of spices" (Song 8:14), make haste to fetch me hence to heaven—this is noble grace, and that which everyone does not come up unto. Indeed, when we are in affliction, and our lives are bitter unto us by reason of many and great trials, difficulties, and temptations, then many are willing to be gone. But this is so far from noble grace that this may be where there is no grace at all. But when the

sun shines upon our tabernacle and sets not, when we live in a paradise of earthly comforts and contentment, then to pant and long to be gone to be with Christ, then to sigh and breathe after the other world, and with a holy impatience to look out for it—this is glorious grace, grace that carries a heavenly odor and savor with it.

Thus I have mentioned some of those more noble and excellent strains of grace for our imitation, which I would have you to labor to come up unto; and the more you come up to these, the more fit you are to live, and the more ready to die.

CHAPTER 10

Pursue Diligence, Communion, Christ's Righteousness, and God's Presence

Wherein further directions are laid down in order to the setting things aright and making him ready for a dying hour.

Seventh, would you indeed have all things right and in order before a dying hour comes? Then be diligent and faithful in the work of God, that work which God in a particular manner has given you to do. We have all our work to do, and that given us from God; we have general work and special work.

(1) We have general work to do: the works of our Christian calling; the work of our salvation, which we are commanded to "work out…with fear and trembling" (Phil. 2:12); the work of faith and the labor of love; the work of mortification, self-denial, and the like.

(2) We have also special work to do: the work of our particular stations and places, work that is incumbent upon us as we stand thus and thus related, being magistrates, or ministers, the masters of families, or the like. For all such relations bring their work and duty with them. And this indeed is properly our own work, and this we should be diligent and faithful in, as ever we would be found ready for a dying hour. Paul had this work to do, and he was diligent and faithful in the discharge of it, which gave him comfort when he came to die: "I am now

ready to be offered, and the time of my departure is at hand. I have fought a good fight, I have finished my course, I have kept the faith: henceforth there is laid up for me a crown of righteousness" (2 Tim. 4:6–8). He had been faithful in the discharge of his work while he lived, and being now to die, he found the comfort and sweetness of it.

Yea, this was that which our Lord Himself comforted Himself with when He was to die, and in the sense of it goes to His Father with boldness for His glory: "I have glorified thee on the earth: I have finished the work which thou gavest me to do" (John 17:4). Indeed, He had a great deal of work given Him by the Father, and He was faithful and punctual in the discharge of it all, which was a comfort to Him now when He was to die. And He Himself tells us, "Blessed is that servant, whom his lord when he cometh shall find so doing," that is faithful and diligent in the discharge of his proper work (Matt. 24:46).

Truly, this is the posture which some (though but a few) are found in; they make conscience to discharge the duty that is incumbent upon them; they say with their Lord, "I must work the works of him that sent me, while it is day: the night cometh, when no man can work" (John 9:4). They see night coming, death coming, judgment coming, eternity coming, and accordingly they desire to lay out their whole souls in the work of God, to live up to the laws of Christ in every relation, and they look upon that day as lost wherein they have not done somewhat for God and their own souls. And how comfortably may such look death in the face when it comes! I have read the life of a holy minister who was seized upon by sickness, which was unto death, while he was preaching the everlasting gospel, and lying a few days sick before he died, a fellow laborer of his, another holy minister, coming to visit him, and seeing death in his face, cried out in some passion, "O dear sir, are you going to heaven from us?" To whom he replied, "Yes, I bless

God, that my Master found me in his work." Truly, might a man have his choice and option, he would have death to find him while he is engaged in the work of God.

O study your own work! Study the work and duty of your Christian calling. Study that work and duty which is incumbent upon you in your particular relations, and beg of God a heart to be diligent in the discharge of one and the other.

Eighth, would you indeed have all right and in order in the matters of your souls, ever a dying hour comes? Then be sure to suffer no distance or estrangement to grow up between God and you, but labor to keep up a constant and intimate acquaintance with Him. "Acquaint now thyself with him, and be at peace" (Job 22:21). The more of a holy intimacy and acquaintance with God we maintain, the more we are at peace with ourselves. And I am sure the more we are at peace in ourselves, the more ready we are for a dying hour.

Woe and alas for us! How often do we let fall our converse and communion with God, and suffer sad distances and estrangements to grow up between Him and us? And indeed, my beloved, it is a sad and amazing thing to think how suddenly and imperceptibly distances and estrangements will grow up between God and a man's soul. For my own part, should I have heard of it only by the hearing of the ear, and had not found it by too many sad and woeful experiences, I could not have believed how suddenly and imperceptibly distances and estrangements will grow up between God and a man's soul—yea, and that after the nearest, liveliest, and most intimate acquaintance and communion with Him, which calls upon us to be very watchful and circumspect as to this thing. And, as you will die with boldness and comfort, let me advise and persuade you to give all diligence to keep up constant intercourse and acquaintance with God, and watch narrowly against all distance between Him and you. Which of us who knows anything of the things of God knows not that we suffer distances and estrangements to grow up between God and us? We cannot tell how, with any tolerable boldness and comfort, to look Him in the face in a duty, or scarcely to think of Him with delight; much less shall we be able to look Him in the face with comfort in death, in case we suffer distances to grow up between Him and us.

Moreover, take this for a sure rule, that the more you are versed in communion with God, and do maintain a holy intimacy and correspondence with Him, the more boldness and comfort you will have when you come to die. Then you will be able to say, "I am now going to be and live forever immediately with that God with whom I have lived with much sweet and intimate communion here; I am now going to converse more fully with Him in heaven, with whom I have enjoyed much sweet converse here on earth." Should death find a man under distances and estrangement between God and him, it must necessarily be uncomfortable unto him; but when there is a holy intimacy kept up between God and the soul, then the soul need not fear or be ashamed to look death and judgment both in the face. "Little children," said John, "abide in him; that, when he shall appear, we may have confidence, and not be ashamed before him at his coming" (1 John 2:28). We are put into Christ by faith at our first conversion, and we abide in Him by further acts of faith and communion.

Now this abiding in Him is the way to have boldness before Him at His coming; therefore, mind this and pray much about this: take heed of distances growing up between God and you, and labor to have those sweet visits, those sweet intercourses of love, those blessed acts of communion kept up between God and you who are prone to be kept up between Him and His watchful, close-walking saints. And in order hereunto, take three or four short hints.

(1) Look upon and esteem converse and communion with God to be (as indeed it is) your highest happiness, both here and in heaven. The highest happiness souls are capable of here is to live in converse and communion with God in such ways as are suitable to this present state, and the highest happiness souls are capable of eternally in heaven is to live in the divine presence, and to see God's face continually, and to lodge forever in the bosom of His love. We may run out to a thousand things, and when we have done all, this will be the highest and indeed the only happiness of souls—namely, to converse with God and to enjoy communion with God; and they who miss of this will miss of all happiness forever. Accordingly, we should prize it and press after it; we should account all things as nothing on this side of God and communion with God in Christ.

The saints of old have done so. "There be many," says David, "that say, Who will shew us any good? LORD, lift thou up the light of thy countenance upon us" (Ps. 4:6), as if he should say, "While others are seeking their happiness from carnal and earthly enjoyments, corn, wine, and oil, the happiness we desire is Thy love, Thy favor, the beaming out of the light of Thy countenance upon our souls." So Psalm 39:7: "Now, Lord, what wait I for? my hope is in thee"; I have done with the streams, as if he should say, "And I desire to cleave wholly to the fountain. I have done with the creatures, of which I have formerly been too fond, and I would now take up my whole rest, solace, and satisfaction in Thee alone." And also, Psalm 73:25–26: "Whom have I in heaven but thee? and there is none upon earth that I desire beside thee. My flesh and my heart faileth: but God is the strength of my heart, and my portion for ever." The same spirit dwelt and acted in Augustine. "All fulness and plenty," says he, "which is not my God, is want and poverty." And again elsewhere, "Thou, Lord, art my God, my happiness; and unto thee, and after thee, do I breathe and sigh day and night." O, my beloved, did we indeed prize communion with God more, we should live more in communion with Him. And this take for a certain truth, that it will never be well with us indeed till we see all in God, and consider that we enjoy all happiness in enjoying communion with Him.

(2) In the close of every day, take a serious view of and diligently consider what has passed between God and you, what transactions there have been between God and your souls that day. There does not a day pass wherein there do not many things pass between God and His people; and he who would prevent distances and estrangements between God and himself should seriously ponder and lay to heart what has passed between God and his soul, what transactions there have been between God and him that day. On the one hand, ponder and consider what has passed from God to you and what His carriage toward you has been; what approaches He has made to you; what intimacies of love; what overtures of communion; what discoveries of Himself and His glory; how far and in what way God has been dealing with your spirits, convincing, enlightening, quickening, or comforting them; what calls He has given you, what myrrh He has dropped upon the handle of the lock; what tastes you have had of His sweetness and grace; what holy impressions He has made upon you, and the like. On the other hand, ponder and consider what has passed from you to God and what your carriages toward Him have been; what acceptation and entertainment you have given Him, making His approaches to you; what value you have put upon His presence and the intimations of His love; how far you have embraced and improved the overtures He made you of further communion with Him; what awe there has been upon you of His holiness and His all-seeing eye; what outgoings of heart there have been found within you after Him; what breathings

of love; what holy longings and desires; what springings and workings of spiritual joy and delight of soul to Him and in Him; what place He has had in your thoughts and contemplations; how far you have lived to Him and upon Him; wherein you have either grieved or delighted His Spirit, and the like.

Thus, in the close of every day, ponder and consider what has passed between God and you, and accordingly deport and demean yourselves before Him. Wherein you have failed or been defective in anything in order to keeping up communion between God and you, be humbled, and set all right by faith and prayer; adore God in His acts of grace and condescension (as to be sure you will find cause so to do); and loathe yourselves for any acts of sin or unkindness, undutifulness, or disrespect that you have been guilty of toward God. This would be a blessed course indeed to prevent distances and estrangements between God and you. This David calls "a communion with his whole heart" and enjoins it as a duty of the highest importance. "Stand in awe, and sin not: commune with your own heart…and be still" (Ps. 4:4). It is what he lived in the practice of (if he were the author of the psalm): "I commune with mine own heart: and my spirit made diligent search" (Ps. 77:6). O be punctual in this work!

(3) Be much conversant, and that with all spiritual diligence, in the ways and duties of communion, those ways wherein God is wont to meet His people and maintain converse and communion with them; and in all of them wait for God and His approaches to you. There are those which we may call ways and duties of communion—ways and duties wherein God and His people do hold converse with each other, wherein God visits and communicates Himself unto His people, and wherein His people may be said to visit God and make out after God—and these are the use of the Word and sacraments, the exercise of prayer, meditation, self-examination, and the like. Now as ever

you would prevent the growing up of distances and estrangements between God and you, see that you are much conversant
in these, and that with a holy and spiritual diligence, waiting
for God and the manifestations of your souls in them; these are
the galleries wherein Christ and His people do take sweet turns
together, the green beds wherein they lie down in the bosom of
each other's love. Therefore, keep up a constant and diligent
attendance on God in these. And in all your attendance on
Him, look after converse with Him; let it be your solemn aim
to converse with Him and see His face, to have a visit, a smile,
a descent of love from Him. I do suppose you to be such as do
and will attend on public ordinances, and wait for God there,
as they waited for the Spirit at Jerusalem. That only then which
I would press you to in this present case shall be, to be much
conversant in prayer and meditation between God and your
own souls, in these two great duties of communion with God:
secret prayer and meditation.

Oh, the loss as to communion with God that we expose
ourselves unto by being no more in prayer and holy meditation! The holy ones of old, and those who have been men
of the highest communion with God, have also been men
of much prayer and great meditation, as I might instance in
David, Daniel, and others. And indeed, their communion
with God came in and was kept up this way. God has told us,
"The prayer of the upright is his delight" (Prov. 15:8). And
Christ speaks of the prayer of His spouse as most pleasing and
delightful to Him: "O my dove, that art in the clefts of the rock,
in the secret places of the stairs, let me see thy countenance,
let me hear thy voice; for sweet is thy voice, and thy countenance is comely" (Song 2:14), as if He should say, "Approach
to me in secret prayer; I will assure you it will be most sweet
and pleasant to Me." And as He thus delights in the prayers
of His people, so He will surely delight them in their prayers

with the visits of His love and communications of His grace, the beaming out of His glory to and upon their souls. He has promised to "make them joyful in [His] house of prayer" (Isa. 56:7); yea, He has promised to perform the whole grace of the new covenant in answer to their prayers (Ezek. 36:27).

Oh, the great things God does for His people, and the sweet communion that is kept up between Him and them, in a way of prayer! I remember a saying of one, "He that is not much in prayer, will never be a man of much excellency." And I may as truly say, "He that is not much in prayer is never like to be a man of much communion with God." And so also for meditation. Oh, how sweet, how heaven-like a duty is that! Oh, how much of God is let out many times to the souls of His people while in meditation! David experienced this: "My soul shall be satisfied as with marrow and fatness; and my mouth shall praise thee with joyful lips: when I remember thee upon my bed, and meditate on thee in the night watches" (Ps. 63:5–6). While he was conversant in this duty of meditation, his soul was filled with joy and satisfaction, as with marrow and fatness. Again: says he, "My meditation of him shall be sweet" (Ps. 104:34). Oh, be much and frequent with God in these ways and duties of communion.

(4) Give Christ His due place and honor in all your strivings after communion with God. Joseph told his brethren they should not see his face unless they brought their brother Benjamin with them; and truly you are not likely to see the face of God in any of the aforementioned ways and duties unless you bring Christ with you and give Him His due place and honor therein—that is to say, unless you eye Him and act in faith upon Him as the only way and medium of communion with God. Christ speaks this at our hands, when He tells us, "I am the way, the truth, and the life: no man cometh unto the Father, but by me" (John 14:6). And by His blood it is that we

have a way opened to us into the holy of holies, access for our persons and prayer into the divine presence (Heb. 10:19–20). Yea, not only has He purchased a liberty and opened a way for us to approach into the presence of God, but having done this by His mediation and intercession it is that any of us comes to God. Hence He is said "to save them to the uttermost that come unto God by him, seeing he ever liveth to make intercession for them" (Heb. 7:25). Indeed, were it not for Christ, none of us could ever hope to see the face of God and live; none of us could ever hope to see one smile of God's face, one embrace of His bosom, any of the least descent and emanation of love from Him. Were it not for Christ, when we come unto God, we should find Him to be a consuming fire, and when He and our souls did meet, it would be as the meeting of devouring fire and withered stubble.

In a word, all communication of grace and love from God to us are by and through Christ; and all the love, the duty, the homage we render to God must be all tendered to Him by and through Christ, if ever we find acceptation with Him. Have Christ, therefore, in your eye in all your approaches unto God, as to Him by whom we "have access by one Spirit unto the Father" (Eph. 2:18). Let the real language of your souls be, "If I have any one smile from God, it must be upon the account of Christ; if He shows Himself pacified toward me, it must be through His blood; if He gives out any grace, any favor, any blessing to me, it will be upon the sole account of His mediation; if ever either my person or services be accepted of the Lord, it must be in and through this Mediator. Moreover, how great soever the distance between God and my soul is, yet Christ can bring me nigh unto Him; and however unworthy of, or unsuitable to, communion with God I am in myself, yet such is His well-pleasedness in Christ, that well-beloved Son of His, that I will hope through Him to find grace in His sight and to be lodged in the bosom of His love." Thus put all the honor upon Christ that is due to Him in this business; this is what is pleasing to the Father. And the more you thus honor Him, the fuller and more constant will your converse and communion with God be.

Ninth, would you indeed have all right and in order for a dying hour? Would you be ready for that last and great work? Then live wholly and constantly upon Christ and His righteousness for your justification and acceptance with God, both living and dying. The more we live out of ourselves upon Christ and His righteousness for justification and acceptance with God, the more ready posture we are in for a dying hour. This indeed is the main thing; and when we have done all that ever we can to deck and adorn ourselves with grace and glorious dispositions, still we must live outside of ourselves, and outside of all those ornaments, upon the naked righteousness of Christ for justification and salvation. This is that which the Scripture calls the readiness of the Lamb's wife: "Let us be glad and rejoice,…for the marriage of the Lamb is come, and his wife hath made herself ready" (Rev. 19:7–8). And wherein that readiness lay, the next words will tell you. "To her was granted that she should be arrayed in fine linen, clean and white: for the fine linen is the righteousness of saints"—that is, the righteousness of Christ imputed to the saints through believing. This is the best robe, mentioned in Luke 15:22, a robe indeed which covers all our nakedness, that beautifies and adorns us, and renders us most amiable in God's eye. Whatsoever spots and blemishes, whatever failings or defects may be upon us, yet these are not seen while God looks upon us as clothed with the righteousness of His Son; and we by faith do live upon that righteousness as the sole matter of our justification and acceptance with Him. And let me tell you, the more clear and distinct the acts of our faith are in carrying us out of ourselves and all self-righteousness, and relying wholly on Christ and His righteousness, the more ready and comfortable posture we are in for a dying hour.

This was the great thing Paul coveted and pressed after to the very last, and which he accounted all things but dung for: "That I may win Christ, and be found in him, not having mine own righteousness, which is of the law, but that which is through the faith of Christ, the righteousness which is of God by faith" (Phil. 3:8–9). He dreaded the thought of being found in anything of his own; he trembled to think of standing upon his own bottom, the bottom of his own worth and righteousness, when he should come to die, and he cleaved entirely unto, and relied wholly upon, Christ and His most perfect righteousness. Oh, let me tell you, Paul had as much, and perhaps more, to have rested upon than ten thousand of us; for gifts, for graces, for privileges, for services, for successes, for sufferings for Christ, he went beyond any mere man who ever lived. And Chrysostom observes of him that he feared nothing but sin; to displease God and to dishonor Him was the only thing that was terrible to him, and the Scripture gives a large and frequent account of his other attainments. But still he rejects all of this; his language is, "None but Christ! None but Christ!" Not but that he also presses after the greatest eminence and exactness in holiness, as you find in the following verses of this third chapter to the Philippians.

Indeed, this is the true spirit of the gospel, to press after the greatest eminence and exactness in holiness—to covet to attain, if possible, unto angelical holiness, and yet under, and after all, to live singly and entirely on Christ alone and His righteousness for justification and acceptation with God. And the more you come to and live in this spirit, the more ready you are for death and a blessed eternity. This was a great part of the ground of the church's rejoicing—"I will greatly rejoice in the LORD, my soul shall be joyful in my God; for he hath clothed me with the garments of salvation, he hath covered me with the robe of righteousness" (Isa. 61:10)—which Chrysostom and others, both ancient and modern, interpret of the righteousness of Christ. And indeed there is no greater ground of rejoicing to a man or woman, whether living or dying, than to be clothed with the robe of the righteousness of Christ. I shall only put you in mind of a saying I have heard from a holy man the day before he died. "My friends," said he, speaking to me and others, "I have walked with God these thirty years, and have enjoyed a good measure of the assurance of His love; but now that I am come to die, I do not place my comfort on any of all these, but on the infinite satisfaction of Jesus Christ." Oh there, there, when we have done all, we must lay the weight and stress of our souls, comfort, salvation, and all! And therefore be sure you live outside of yourselves upon Christ.

It is a great saying Luther has to this purpose: "Lord Jesus," said he, "Thou art my righteousness, and I am Thy sin. Thou tookest mine [meaning his sin] and Thou gavest me Thine [meaning His righteousness]; Thou tookest that which Thou wast not, and Thou gavest me that which I was not," intending the exchange that Christ had made with him, giving him His righteousness for his sin. O let this be the language of our souls to Christ, so shall we be found ready when a dying hour comes.

Tenth, would you indeed die with comfort? Then beg God to stand by you and give you actual grace in a dying hour, and make it one of your great works to treasure up many prayers for this beforehand. When you have done all, should God withdraw His presence and the influences of His grace and love from you when you come to die, death would be in a great measure uncomfortable to you. But if God will be with you, if God will stand by you, if He will vouchsafe you the influences and communications of His grace in a dying hour, then how will your souls triumph over death! This indeed will sweeten death. They are great words of David in Psalm 23:4, "Though I walk through the valley of the shadow of death, I will fear no evil: for thou art with me." Having the presence of God with him, he was not, he would not, be afraid, even in the very valley of the shadow of death. Truly, without the presence of God, we cannot live comfortably, whatsoever our attainments in grace have been, yet if God withdraw His presence from us, we can do nothing, we cannot perform the least duty, we cannot resist the least temptation, we cannot grapple with the least corruption, nor carry through, as we ought, the least difficulty. Much less shall we be able to die with comfort if God withdraw; therefore, I say, beg God to stand by you in a dying hour. Let it be your daily prayer to God:

(1) That He would be with you in the difficulties of life.

(2) That He would not leave you in the conflicts and agonies of death. And indeed we should not pass that day wherein we do not treasure up one prayer for this beforehand; and thus doing, God will not leave us, God will not fail us in that last and great difficulty—at least He will not leave us in point of grace. Our Lord Himself was left in the agonies of death by the Father, in point of comfort, which put Him to that cry, "Why hast thou forsaken me?" But He was not left by Him in point of grace; still a spirit of faith and holiness acted in Him, and therefore, though forsaken, He cries out, "My God, my God." If possible, in conformity to our Head, we should be left in that hour in point of comfort, yet if we carry ourselves as we ought, we shall not be left in point of grace; and if we be not left in point of grace, all will be well, though not so sweet and joyous with us as otherwise it would be. And thus I have given you these more particular directions in order to prepare for a dying hour; which if you live up to, you may not only live above the fear of death but also in the joyful expectation of it daily.

CHAPTER 11

Death for the Believer

Being a consolatory conclusion of the whole discourse, containing encouragements against the fear of death unto all such as are found in the practice of the foregoing directions.

Now for a conclusion of the whole matter. Upon all that has been declared, soul, let me ask you one question: Do you indeed see your particular concern in this business? Do you so see it as really to make it your great work and solicitude while living to set all things right and make all things ready for a dying hour? Some there are who are so happy as so to do; and are you one of them? Then why should you fear death? Yea, why should not you exalt and your heart leap within you at the sight and thought of its approach? True, it is a dark entry, but it leads to a fair and stately palace, even the Father's house. It is a rough and difficult passage, but it sets you safe on shore in a large and fat land. True, it carries with it somewhat of a black, lowering, and ghastly aspect to nature (and nature may at first possibly be startled and recoil at the sight of it), but open the eye of your faith and behold it in the glass of the gospel; view it in the death of your Lord and Head, and it will not appear half so terrible. Yea, you will find it to be not so much an enemy as a friend; not as a king of terror but rather as a king of comforts; not as an object to be dreaded and trembled at, but rather to be rejoiced in and triumphed over by you. It will appear to be not loss but gain: "For to me…to die is gain," says Paul (Phil. 1:21). Yea, it will be your great gain, it will be the end of all your misery and the perfecting of all your happiness; and the truth is, we are never perfectly happy until death comes. But for your further encouragement, I shall in a few particulars show you what death, come when it will, does and will do for such as make ready for its coming.

(1) Death, whenever it comes, will translate your ready soul, from earth to heaven, from a strange land to your own home and Father's house, and will not this be a kindness? As for this world, what is it to the poor saints but a strange land? Heaven is their home and country, hence they have confessed and do confess themselves to be strangers and pilgrims upon earth (Heb. 11:13). And the psalmist, in the word immediately foregoing my text (Ps. 39:12), owns it to God, "I am a stranger with thee, and a sojourner." Yea, this world is not only a strange land but a waste, howling wilderness to such, wherein they live among wild beasts, lions, bears, wolves, tigers, and the like. Lusts within and devils without, ready daily to devour them; but now when death comes, it carries them off from this strange land, this waste, howling wilderness, to their own home and country, which is heaven—yea, to their Father's house, there to live with Him, to enjoy His presence, and to adore His grace. "We know," says the apostle, "that if our earthly house of this tabernacle [speaking of the body] were dissolved, we have a building with God, an house not made with hands, eternal in the heavens" (2 Cor. 5:1). And you know how Christ speaks: "In my Father's house are many mansions: if it were not so, I would have told you" (John 14:2), and thither does death carry you when it comes.

Oh sweet! Oh my beloved! To go home, to go to our Father's house and to possess our mansion there, that mansion which our dear Lord and Head is gone before to prepare for us, how sweet is this to think of? And how many deaths may it sweeten? Suppose one of you were some thousand miles distant from home, country, and comforts, and you were in a waste, howling wilderness among lions and bears, ready to devour you, a wide sea also being between home and you; and suppose that a ship should come and take you on board and in a short time set you down in your own country and among all your friends and comforts. Would not this be a kindness? Why, this is your case here, O you preparing souls, and this is the kindness death does for you when it comes; while here you are ten thousand miles distant from your home and country, your friends and comforts, and in a waste, howling wilderness, but death, that swift sailor, comes, and in a moment sets you down in heaven, your home and country. O how welcome should it then be to you!

(2) Death, whenever it comes, will carry you from trouble to rest, from a tempestuous sea to a quiet haven, there to lie at an eternal anchor in the bosom of your sweet Lord. This world ever was and ever will be a place of trouble to the people of God. Sure I am, Christ has told us, "In the world ye shall have tribulation" (John 16:33). And who of us does not find this to be true? This world is a tempestuous sea, wherein the waves lift up themselves, and the poor saints are afflicted and tossed with tempests and oftentimes not comforted (Isa. 54:11). We read in Jonah 1:13 that "the sea wrought, and was tempestuous," and the mariners strove to row hard to get the ship to shore. And truly, thus it is often in the case in hand, the sea of this world is tempestuous, it works, and the poor saints strive to row hard to get safe to shore; yea, as we read in Acts 27:14,

a tempestuous east wind arose and beat upon Paul and others in the ship with him, which was ready to break all in pieces!

So truly the saints in this world do meet with tempestuous winds not a few, which beat upon them and are ready to split all and sink all; and now when death comes, those storms are made a calm, and they (I mean the saints) are brought into the desired haven. Death sets them at rest: "There," says Job, speaking of the grave, "the weary be at rest" (Job 3:17). Death sends the body to rest; it frees it from all sensible sufferings. When death comes, your weak body, your sick body, your pained body, your consumptive body, shall have its dismission to rest. And death sends the soul to rest, that rest in God and with God. "Blessed are the dead which die in the Lord from henceforth: Yea, saith the Spirit, that they may rest from their labours" (Rev. 14:13). And you have, I think, both together in one Scripture, Isaiah 57:2, where speaking of the righteous, it is said, they "shall enter into peace: they shall rest in their beds." Hence we read that "there remaineth therefore a rest to the people of God" (Heb. 4:9). Indeed, it remains; it is not here. But when death comes, that sets them down in this remaining rest.

O what a kindness must this be? Rest! O how sweet is rest? How desirable is rest? And rest too after long and hard labor and trouble? How sweet is rest to a laboring man who has worked hard all the day? How sweet is rest to the weary traveler who has gone a long and dirty journey? How sweet is rest to the solicitous mariner, and how welcome is the harbor to him, especially after having been long tossed and beaten with storms and tempests? And how sweet will rest be to the poor, troubled, tempted, laboring, traveling saint, whose whole life has been little else but trouble, labor, and sore travel, who here could scarce all his days find a resting place for the sole of his foot, the world as to him being covered with a deluge?

(3) Death, whenever it comes, will turn your conflicts into victory, this *Aceldama*, or field of blood (for such is this world), into a mount of triumph, a throne of glory! What is this world but an *Aceldama*, a field of blood to the poor saints? Sure I am this life is little else but a perpetual war and conflict with lusts, with devils, with afflictions, and with temptations; hence it is called a fight, a warfare, and the like. And the enemies which they in this warfare are to grapple with are formidable enemies. "We wrestle not," says the apostle, "against flesh and blood, but against principalities, against powers, against the rulers of the darkness of this world, against spiritual wickedness" (Eph. 6:12). We wrestle not with flesh and blood—that is, with men or anything that is frail and weak; no, we have more potent and formidable enemies to deal with; we wrestle and conflict with devils, who are potent, subtle, and indefatigable. "Enemies," as Calvin observes upon the place, "which wound before they appear, and kill before they are seen; enemies which deal not only by force and power, but who are dreadful, crafty and subtle, yea, enemies which have fiery darts to cast at us," as afterward he speaks. And for my own part, I think it were well for us, if these were the worst enemies we had to grapple and conflict with; but there are legions of lusts within (which I look upon to be worse enemies), which we do and must wrestle with (internal enemies are in many respects the worst: these "war against the soul" [1 Peter 2:11]). And were it not for these, all the devils in hell could do us no hurt.

Thus, this life is to the saints a warfare, a conflict; and oh the wounds, the bruises, the bloodshed which they are exposed to in this war! Now their peace and then their grace, now their comforts and then their consciences, are sorely wounded, and they lie bleeding for days, and weeks, and months together; yea, sometimes like him that was traveling from Jerusalem to Jericho, they were wounded and left half dead, and did not the good Samaritan pass by, taking compassion on them, and pour in of his wine and oil, his blood and spirit into their wounds, they would soon be wholly dead.

Well, but now when death comes, that puts an end to this war and sets them all down upon a throne of triumph. "To him that overcometh," says Christ, "will I grant to sit with me in my throne, even as I also overcame, and am set down with my Father in his throne" (Rev. 3:21). When death comes, then you begin an eternal triumph with Christ, then the palm will be put into your hands and you shall triumphantly cry, "Victory, victory forever." O how sweet will this be! How sweet is the victory to a soldier that has been long and hard put to it in the battle? And indeed, the harder the battle, the more glorious the triumph. It is a sweet and great saying which I have read in Augustine to this purpose: "The conqueror," says he, "triumphs, and unless he had fought he had never conquered. And by how much the greater his danger and difficulty was in the battle, by so much the greater is his joy in the triumph." Not only will death set you upon a mount of triumph, but know for your encouragement, the sharper your conflicts and warfare have been here, the more glorious will your triumph be when death shall set you upon the throne.

(4) Death, whenever it comes, will change your bondage into liberty, your spiritual thraldom into glorious freedom; and is not this a kindness? Poor soul, one thing here which you bleed and groan under is that spiritual bondage and thraldom which you lie under. And indeed this world is no other than a prison, a dungeon, a house of bondage to you, the land of your captivity. Here you lie in chains and fetters, the chains and fetters of sin and guilt. Yea, and the iron sometimes enters into your spirit. Hence we read of the "bondage of corruption" (Rom. 8:21), which indeed is the sorest bondage in the world, a worse bondage ten thousand times than that which

Israel groaned and sighed under in Egypt, who yet were made "to serve with rigour" and whose lives were made "bitter with hard bondage" (Ex. 1:13–14).

Truly, this lust and the other lusts, this corruption and other corruptions, are as so many Egyptians, cruel taskmasters, which make you serve with rigor, and your life bitter to you with hard bondage. And O how do you groan and sigh under the bondage of a proud, dead, hard, carnal, unbelieving heart, a heart bent to backsliding from God! And indeed, who that is sensible of it can but groan under it? This drew that heavy groan from Paul, and bitter outcry, "O wretched man that I am!" (Rom. 7:24), says he. Why, Paul, what's the matter? "Oh," says he, "I find a law in my members warring against the law in my mind, and bringing me into captivity to the law of sin, and that I am by sin brought into captivity to sin, and I have a body of sin and death lying heavy upon me, heavier than a mountain of brass or iron; and who can but groan?" And as it was with him, so it is with all the saints in their measure.

Well, but when death comes, that will turn all this your bondage into liberty, yea, into "the glorious liberty of the children of God" (Rom. 8:21), yea, that will turn again this your captivity. And O how sweet will that be? You have some little tastes of this liberty here, for "where the Spirit of the Lord is, there is liberty" (2 Cor. 3:17), and the tastes of it are sweet, very sweet. But O how sweet will the full enjoyment of it be? Paul breaks out into praises in the faith of it beforehand: "I thank God through Jesus Christ" (Rom. 7:25). O soul, how should this make you long for death? Can a prison, can a house of bondage, can a state of thraldom be pleasant to you? Can you be well pleased to lie in chains and fetters of sin and guilt? Should you not rather welcome that which alone would work your deliverance?

(5) Death, whenever it comes, will be the death of all your sins and the perfection of all your graces. And will not that be a kindness? Poor saint, how do you here bleed and groan under the sense of the life and vigor of your sins, on the one hand, and the weakness and imperfection of your graces, on the other hand? Yea, how great are the conflicts, the holy contentions of your spirit, to kill and bring down the one and to quicken and perfect the other? How do you, with the holy apostle of old, "forgetting those things which are behind, and reaching forth unto those things which are before…press toward the mark for the prize of the high calling of God in Christ Jesus" (Phil. 3:13–14)?

Oh the watchings, the warnings, the wrestlings of your soul for more grace, more holiness, more victory over and cleansing from sin! Oh, the many prayers and tears, sighs and groans that you pour out between God and your soul in order hereunto! These things are the business of your life; yea, and after all, sin is still strong and lively, and grace is still weak and imperfect, the sense of which breaks your heart almost and makes you go mourning all the day long. What, daily cleansing yourself and yet still unclean? Daily perfecting holiness yet still imperfect? O how sad is this! Well, but soul, when death comes, things will be strangely altered with you. That will do that for you in one moment which you by a whole life of prayers, tears, faith, watching, warring, laboring, could not do; it will make you perfect. Hence those above are said to be so: "The spirits of just men made perfect" (Heb. 12:23); "that which is perfect is come, then that which is in part shall be done away" (1 Cor. 13:10). Perfect grace, perfect holiness.

Now there is much lacking in your faith, your love, your obedience, your humility, your heavenliness, your joy and delight in God; but death, when it comes, will make up all in a moment. Yea, now you are stained and defiled with sin, and this lust and the other lust stirs, and works, and wars within you; but when death comes, that will purge away all. Death is the saint's only perfect cleanser through Christ. Indeed, it is said of wicked men and hypocrites that their iniquity "shall lie down with [them] in the dust" (Job 20:11), which is a dreadful word indeed. Death does not kill their sins. No, they live in the grave; they go with them into the other world and will there live in them forever, which will be a great part of their torment. It will be indeed (however they may now think of it) the one half of hell. For what is hell but sin at the highest and wrath at the hottest? But though it be thus with wicked ones, yet it is otherwise with the saints; death through the grace of Christ will forever put an end to your sin and perfect your graces. O sweet! Who would not welcome death!

(6) Death, whenever it comes, will set you above all afflictive distances between God, Christ, the Comforter, and you will set down your soul in the full, constant, and immediate vision and fruition of all forever; and is not this sweet? Poor saint, here you complain that God is a stranger to you, and "as a wayfaring man that turneth aside to tarry for a night." You have only now and then a short visit from Him (Jer. 14:8). You complain that your beloved withdraws Himself and is gone (Song 5:6). You complain that the Comforter that should relieve your soul is far from you (Lam. 1:16). You complain of many sad and woeful distances from God, and of the lowliness of your communion, and well you may! For indeed, how little a portion is there here seen or enjoyed of Him by you?

Well, but when death comes, that will lift you above all those distances between God and you, Christ and you, and set you down in the full, constant, and immediate vision and fruition of Him forever, the thoughts of which made Paul, and others, to desire to be gone and to choose death rather than life: "We are always confident," says he, "knowing that, whilst we are at home in the body, we are absent from the Lord: (For we walk by faith, not by sight:) We are confident, I say, and willing rather to be absent from the body, and to be present with the Lord" (2 Cor. 5:6–8). Notice that Paul enjoyed as much of God and Christ here as most did, and yet all that communion he enjoyed here he accounted as no communion to that which he should enjoy after death; while we are present "in the body," says he, that is, while we live in this world, "we are absent from the Lord," absent from God and Christ. Our communion here is but distance and estrangement, so low and inconstant is it in comparison of what we know we shall enjoy after death. And therefore, says he, we had rather be absent from the body, we had rather be gone hence, and be present with the Lord. Death will bring us to another sort of kind presence and enjoyment of God and Christ than here we shall ever be able to reach unto.

Alas! All we enjoy of God and Christ here is but as an earnest; so the apostle speaks in the verse foregoing: "He that hath wrought us for the selfsame thing is God, who also hath given unto us the earnest of the Spirit" (2 Cor. 5:5). But when death comes, we shall enjoy the full inheritance. All we enjoy here is but as the firstfruits, we that "have the firstfruits of the Spirit," says the apostle (Rom. 8:23). But when death comes, we shall have the full vintage, full communications of love, full manifestations of light and life and glory, "fulness of joy...pleasures for evermore" in the divine presence (Ps. 16:11), full embraces of Christ's bosom, full views of His face, full visions of His glory. Death, when it comes, will bring us to the beatifical vision, which is all good and happiness in one: "Blessed are the pure in heart: for they shall see God" (Matt. 5:8). They do see God now; they see Him by faith, and those sights of Him are sweet, glorious, soul-ravishing, and trans-forming sights. But after death they shall have other sights of

Him, such sights of Him as will even infinitely surpass all that they ever had or were capable of here. Here they "see through a glass, darkly"—that is, they have but low, obscure, mediate sights of Him; they see and enjoy but little of Him. But when death comes, then they shall see Him "face to face"—that is, fully, clearly, immediately (1 Cor. 13:12).

The sum is, as a learned man gives it to us, that "in this life we have but slow and slender sights and enjoyments of God in comparison of what we shall see, know, and enjoy of him in eternal life." Here they see but His back parts, as God said to Moses; but when death comes they shall see His face—that is, His glory. Here they see Him but negatively, as it were; but there, they will see what He is, "We shall see him as he is" (1 John 3:2), in all His glorious excellencies and perfections. In short, they shall then have such sights and enjoyments of God and Christ as shall eternally fill, delight, solace, satisfy, and set at rest their souls forever, such sights and enjoyments as shall so solace and satisfy them as that there shall be no room for the least tittle or iota of a desire forever. Yea, such sights and enjoyments as shall so satisfy them as to leave them under an utter impossibility of ever turning aside from them to anything else, and so an eternal impossibility of sinning. O how sweet must this be! And indeed the schoolmen, I find, and others from them, give this as one reason why the saints in heaven are impeccable, because the sight and enjoyment they have of God there is so full and satisfying as that they cannot turn aside to anything else. O welcome death that brings us to those sights, those enjoyments of God, the chief good!

(7) Death, whenever it comes, will bring you to and set you down in the enjoyment of an eternal Sabbath. And oh how sweet is this! "There remaineth therefore a rest [the word is, a Sabbath] to the people of God" (Heb. 4:9). But when shall they enjoy it? Why, truly, when death comes, that will enter

them upon it immediately; upon the night of death dawns the eternal Sabbath. True, the saints enjoy a Sabbath here, and the Sabbath to them is the sweetest and ablest day in all the week. It is a day of joy and holy feasting to their souls, and O how many times do your souls long for it? But alas, these Sabbaths have an end; but the Sabbath that death will set them down in will be an eternal Sabbath: an eternal Sabbath wherein they shall be employed in the highest acts of worship and adoration, even love, praise, admiration, and hallelujahs forever; wherein there will be no weariness, no faintness; wherein there shall be no intermission, no going to duties and breaking off again, as here we do. But a whole eternity shall be employed in acts of divine worship and adoration, wherein there shall be no deadness, no dullness, no spiritual indispositions, no unsuitableness in us to those high and holy exercises which this Sabbath will be filled with. But our souls shall be perfectly suited to and fitted for those glorious employs wherein not a few only (and those some saints and some sinners, some good and some bad) shall join together in acts of worship, but an innumerable company of both saints and angels and those all perfectly holy (Heb. 12:22–24).

O how sweet and glorious will this be! It is a great saying which I have read in a worthy divine: "Sabbaths here are comfortable," says he, "and we have tasted some sweet, some comfort, in some Sabbaths; but taste all the comfort that ever you had in all the Sabbaths you have enjoyed here, and all will be nothing to the comforts and sweetness of the eternal Sabbath." Alas! The perpetual Sabbath that shall be hereafter, that will be the accomplishment of all these Sabbaths, how sweet then must that be! O you saints of God, lift up your heads; death will set you down in this Sabbath. How have some of us longed sometimes for the coming of the Sabbath! And how have we grieved when it has been gone? Well, but when death comes, that will bring you to a Sabbath that shall never end. It is a sweet saying of Augustine, "There," says he, speaking of heaven, "is the great Sabbath, a Sabbath that hath no evening, no end, on which we shall rest and behold, behold and love, love and praise for ever."

Oh blessed be God for this Sabbath! And blessed be God that death, when it comes, shall bring us to this Sabbath. Well then, fear not death, dread not death, but be found diligent and faithful in the use of the helps prescribed for the preparing of your souls for it, and then it will greatly befriend you whenever it comes, and you may exult and rejoice in it.

I shall now conclude, but I must first beg all who read this plain discourse deeply and frequently to consider and contemplate these things.

(1) Every day seriously consider and contemplate the exceeding worth of your souls and the great things they are capable of. It is sad to think what low thoughts the most of men have of their souls; they are content to sell their souls, to lose their souls, to damn their souls, and all for a lust, for a little of this world, a little carnal, sensual pleasure and delight here, which is but for a moment. That rebuke which Augustine gave one is due to most: "How comes it to pass that among all the good things you will let nothing be in an ill case, but yourself, your soul!" Truly the most of men are solicitous to have all well but their souls; they will have it go well with their bodies, their names, their estates, their families, but their souls they mind not. But, my beloved, I beseech you, think deeply and frequently of the worth of your souls and the concerns of them. O it is your soul that is your principal part! Christ, who best knew the worth of souls, tells you that the whole world is nothing to one soul and that the gain of the one cannot recompense the loss of the other, no, not in the least (Matt. 16:26). And you know what a price He was pleased to pay for

souls, even His own blood, His precious blood, life and all (1 Peter 1:19). Besides, there are two things which speak the soul to be a thing of unspeakable worth and value: its vast capacity and its absolute immortality.

(i) The capacity of the soul speaks its worth. O what great things is the soul of man capable of! There is a kind of infiniteness, as a worthy divine observes, in the soul of man. It is capable of even an infinite happiness, or an infinite misery; it is capable of eternal life or eternal death; it is capable of inconceivable communications, both of love and wrath, and must one day be filled with the one or the other of them; it is capable of knowing God, or bearing His image, of enjoying glorious communication with Him, yea, of the living God's own life, and in a participation of His own blessedness. Look at whatever the angels enjoy, look at whatever the human soul of Christ enjoys, that the soul is capable of the enjoyment of. Sinner, O how precious does this speak it to be! And how great should your concern be for it while days and seasons last! Contemplate it therefore a little, and say, "O how precious is my soul, and what great things is it capable of? And it being so, why do I take up in such low, poor, dungy, drossy things, as the best of sin and this world are?"

(ii) The immortality of the soul argues its worth. The soul never dies. It is indeed but, as it were, a spark, a beam of God's own immortality breathed into the body; at least there is a stamp and impress thereof upon it. The body, that dies, that returns to dust; but the soul, that lives, that goes to God (Eccl. 12:7). As the mortality of the body, as the learned man observes, so the immortality of the soul is here asserted. Besides, Abraham, Isaac, and Jacob, with the rest of the good old patriarchs and the servants of God, who died long since, are notwithstanding living still, so Christ argues you know (Matt. 22:32); that is, their souls live, as indeed do the souls of all who are gone hence. Their souls will live either in happiness or in misery, with God or devils, and so must yours and mine, sinner. When our bodies shall be eaten by the worms, our souls will live either in heaven or in hell. O think of this: daily contemplate and say, "I have a soul within me that must live forever, and that as filled with even an infinite happiness or misery; I have a soul within me that is capable of unspeakable joys or inconceivable torments, and in the one or the other it will, it must, live forever. Why then am I not more concerned for it?"

(2) Seriously contemplate and daily keep your spirits on the thoughts of the wonderful weight and importance of eternity, the greatest concern of the other world. O eternity, eternity! O vast, great, boundless eternity! How shall I speak of you? How are my thoughts lost, and my spirit overwhelmed, when I set myself to contemplate how great, how weighty a thing you are? An endless, boundless, bottomless state; a state that admits of neither change, pause, nor an end forever; a state of inconceivable happiness or misery. Happiness in the enjoyment, or misery in the loss of, and banishment from God and Christ forever. Happiness in the fruition of infinite love, or misery in the revelation of infinite wrath, one of which every soul must be the object of forever.

Eternity! Such is the weight of it in itself that indeed we know not how to conceive of it. Everything but eternity has an end at last. So innumerable as the stars of heaven are, yet there is a last star, and the number of them has an end, though we cannot reach it. So innumerable as the sands on the seashore are, yet there is a last grain of sand, and the number of them has an end, could we reach it. So numerous as the piles of grass, which are now, and from the creation of the world have been, and to the end of the world shall be are, yet there is an end of the number of them, could we reach it; there is a last pile, a last spire of grass. So innumerable as the grains of corn in all the harvests that ever were, or shall be, are, yet the number of them has an end, though we cannot reach it, and there is a last grain. So innumerable as all the drops of rain that ever did fall, or shall fall, upon the earth, from the creation to the end of the world, are, yet there is a last drop, yea, and that though all the drops contained in the wide and deep sea be added thereunto. So innumerable as the children of men have been, are, and shall be, to the end of all things, so innumerable as all the hairs of the head of them all have been, are, and will be. So innumerable as all the thoughts of the hearts of all throughout all ages have been, are, and will be. So innumerable as all the brutes and animals, which both the earth and the sea have brought forth, do, and will bring forth, are, and will be, yet still the number of them has an end, could we reach it; and there is a last man, a last hair, a last thought, a last animal. Should all the vast body of the heavens, which our eyes behold, be fully written with figures by the hand of an angel, yet the number of those figures would have an end, and there would be a last figure.

But as for eternity, that has no end. Could all those vast numbers aforementioned be put together into one, who could in the least conceive of the thousand thousandth part of it? Yet all this were nothing to eternity, no, not a thousand thousandth part of it. Thus, eternity is inconceivably weighty in itself, and it is eternity indeed that puts weight into all other things. It is eternity that puts weight into the future judgment. What were that judgment but that it is eternal judgment (Heb. 6:2)? It is eternity that puts weight indeed into the happiness and joys of heaven. What were that happiness, and those joys, were they not eternal? Hence it is called eternal life, eternal glory, a never fading crown, an everlasting kingdom, joy and pleasure forevermore. So the Scripture speaks of it as that which is its crown and perfection; hence we read of being forever with the Lord (1 Thess. 4:17). To be with the Lord is sweet. Peter found it so; all the saints in their measure find it so here. But to be with the Lord forever, that makes it infinitely sweet indeed. Thus and thus forever in the bosom of my Father's love; and there forever in the views of my Redeemer's glory; and there forever joined with an innumerable company of angels in loving, praising, admiring, adoring, and singing hallelujahs to God and the Lamb; and this forever to be fully swallowed up in the divine life, the divine will, the divine presence, the divine fulness; and this forever to be set above all sin, to be delivered from an unavoidable necessity of sinning, to an absolute impossibility of sinning.

O how sweet, how glorious is this! This one word, *eternity* or *forever*, is that which puts great sweetness into it. Again, it is eternity that indeed puts weight into the miseries and torments of the damned. What were the fire of hell were it not unquenchable fire? What were the worm there were it not a never-dying worm? When the Scripture would speak of the exceeding greatness and severity of those torments, it is in this language: "Their worm dieth not, and the fire is not quenched" (Mark 9:44). There miseries and torments are eternal, and indeed hell would be no hell, in comparison, had it not eternity in it. Most weighty is the meditation which I have read in a learned and holy man to this purpose: "O eternity! Eternity! O never-ending eternity! O eternity, that can be measured by no space of time, that can be perceived or apprehended by no human intellect or understanding! How inconceivably do you augment the torments of the damned!" And but a few lines after he again cries out, "O eternity! Eternity! You, and you alone, do aggravate the torments, the punishments of the damned beyond all measure."

Heavy is the punishment of the damned because of its sharpness, its extensiveness, its universality, there being all plagues and punishments in it; but, says he, it is most heavy because of its eternity. O it is this indeed that makes it intolerably great and heavy. Oh! Not only to be banished from God and Christ, to be driven from the beatifical vision, but to be banished and driven from hence forever. Oh doleful! To be in the flames, to suffer the vengeance of eternal fire, to be sinning, and always bearing the punishment of sin, and all this forever! O this makes it out of measure heavy, thus, and always thus, under the wrath of God, and forever so! This puts weight into it. Thus you see a little of the weight of eternity. O contemplate it daily!

(3) Consider and contemplate how doleful a thing it will be to miscarry forever, and on the other hand, what a wide door of mercy there is open to you and the fair opportunity you have of making a blessed provision for your souls and eternity.

(i) Consider and contemplate how doleful a thing it will be to miscarry forever, to perish eternally. The more worth there is in the soul, and the greater weight there is in eternity, the more doleful it will be to perish or miscarry. As to the interest of them to miscarry in our estate, in our trade, in our name, in the change of our condition in this world, or the like, this is sad, and sinks many; but O what is this to the miscarriage of the soul forever! What is this to miserable eternity, to the loss of God, of Christ, of the Comforter, of heaven, and eternal life? What is this to the wrath of God, to the vengeance of eternal fire, to utter darkness, to blackness of darkness forever?

To have infiniteness and eternity combine against you to make you miserable and to be forever as miserable as infiniteness and eternity can make you (as assuredly you will, in case you neglect to make provision for your souls and the future life), O how dreadful, how doleful will this be! And what bitter lamentations will it fill you with forever! Did Esau weep when he had lost his birthright? And did Lysrmachus upbraid himself, and bewail his folly, for parting with his kingdom for a draught of water? O then how will you weep and wail, and even tear and torment yourselves forever, for your sin and folly, when you shall find that for a little of this world; for the satisfaction of a lust; for a few drossy pleasures and sensual delights; or perhaps through a mere sloth of spirit, you have lost your souls and have plunged yourselves into an infinite ocean of eternal woe and misery, whence there is no redemption forever for you! Pray lay that Scripture to heart now: "Depart from me," says Christ, "all ye workers of iniquity" (Luke 13:27).

Depart; this doom will pass at last upon every unrepenting, unbelieving sinner, every soul that makes not ready for a dying hour. Well, and what then? "There shall be weeping and gnashing of teeth, when you shall see Abraham, Isaac, and Jacob and all the Prophets in the Kingdom of God, and you thrust out." When you shall see such and such lodged safe in heaven, in the bosom of Christ, and yourselves shut out, and not only so, but cast into outer darkness, as you have it added (Matt. 8:12)—when you shall see yourselves shut in the infernal pit and there sealed up under God's eternal wrath—O then you will weep and gnash your teeth indeed! Then your own conscience will be eternally a second hell to you, tearing and tormenting your souls in the remembrance of your sin and folly, in neglecting to prepare for, and make sure of, a better state. Think of these things before it be too late.

(ii) Consider and contemplate what a wide door of mercy there is open to you, and what a fair opportunity God gives you, to make blessed provision for your souls and eternity. What shall I say? Why, sirs, the way of salvation is made plain to you, and you are daily called to the marriage supper of the Lamb; the great King of heaven invites you to come and partake of this gospel feast. By one and another servant of His which He sends to you, He lets you know that all things are ready, all that your souls can need to make them happy forever. Christ is ready, and in Him life is ready, grace is ready, peace is ready, pardon is ready, a complete righteousness for your justification and acceptance with God is ready, heaven is ready, salvation is ready, and withal He bids you come. Yea, He earnestly importunes and solicits you to come and feast your souls upon these things; He freely and frequently offers Himself and all to you, entreating your acceptance. Yea more, He opens the arms of His love to you, assuring you of most cordial welcome and ready reception, notwithstanding all your sins and miscarriages. "Him that cometh to me I will in no wise cast out" (John 6:37).

"Let him be who and what he will, a young or an old sinner, a small or a great sinner, a sinner that has stood it out against Me a little or a long time, I will not cast him out. My grace is free, My fullness is large and sufficient, My blood is precious, and this has an infinite virtue in it. My Spirit is powerful and efficacious; I am every way mighty to save, able to 'save to the uttermost all that come to God by Me.' Yea, it is My work and business to save; My Father sealed and sent Me for that end, and for that end came I into the world, and there did and suffered such things as I did. And I may not, I will not, cast off any poor soul that will come and partake of Me and My fullness and that would fain be helped on toward life and blessedness."

This is really the language of Christ to poor sinners; yea more, He sends His Spirit to enlighten, to convince, to persuade, to draw and allure them, and He does move in them and strive with them. O what a wide door of mercy is there here open to you! And how fair is your opportunity of preparing for, and making sure of, a blessed eternity? Oh! Accordingly as you love your souls and would live forever, come in to Christ, come and apply, and improve Him in a way of believing, for the good of your eternal souls. In His strength set upon repenting. Believing, work the work of your souls and eternity; and your day being so bright, as indeed it is, labor to know the things of your peace in your day, lest neglecting them Christ speedily say of you, as once with tears in His eyes He did of neglectful Jerusalem, "If thou hadst known, even thou, at least in this thy day, the things which belong unto thy peace! but now they are hid from thine eyes" (Luke 19:42).

I have done. I'll close all with that holy wish for you, my dear congregation, and myself, that Augustine was wont to make for himself, and his people, namely, "That as they had been often crowded together to worship God in that earthly temple, wherein he preached, so they might eternally live together in the heavenly temple above." So my wish and desire is that we, my beloved, you and I, who have often been thronged and crowded together in an earthly house, may live together eternally, and eternally adore God together in our Father's house above. And if we shall never preach and pray, hear, and sing together more on earth (as I am apt to think we shall not), yet that we may praise, love, and admire God, and sing hallelujahs to Him forever together in heaven. Amen, amen.

A Proposition for the More Profitable Improvement of Burials by Giving of Books

That great stupidity that is on the generality of mankind concerning their mortality does manifest the usefulness of books of this subject. For although men know that, by reason of the first transgression, it is appointed for all men once to die; though the principles of this natural life (by which it is upheld) are so weak that they cannot support it long; though there are many internal causes that, as secret mines, may soon blow up men, even of the strongest constitution, and many external causes, as a tile from a house or the stumbling of a horse, that may soon cast men into the grave; though there are continual representations and spectacles of mortality in which men, as in a glass, behold their natural fate; and though men always carry about them the symptoms of mortality, and the marks of death, yet they generally live as if they should never die. In small villages where instances of mortality are very rare, there the inward thought of the hearts seems to be that they and their houses shall continue forever, and their dwelling places to all generations. In populous towns and cities, there the commonness takes away the sense of mortality. And how sad is it to behold the unsuitable carriage of the generality of Christians at funerals! Those opportunities are usually spent in unprofitable chat, in mirth, in eating and drinking (and that sometimes to excess), and thus the house of mourning is turned into the house of mirth and feasting.

To cure this evil frame, we have thought good to propound that which we find to be the wish of the generality of pious persons—namely, that books of this nature may be given at burials instead of rings, gloves, biscuits, wine, and so on (either to persons invited or to such godly poor people as may be thought most convenient, who are not able to buy them as their last legacy, and the relations of the deceased may have a small abridgement of his or her life and character printed in two or three leaves, to bind up with the books, for a small charge, and what number they think most convenient to dispose of for the benefit of the living, being their last act of charity to the poor (if they shall think convenient). Reading and meditation would be much more decent at such sad solemnities than eating and drinking and putting on of ornaments. Books of this subject would make people mind the present instance of mortality and affect them with such devout meditations as these: "Lord! This tragedy that is now acting on our deceased friend must before long (God knows how soon) be acted on us all; our breath is ready to perish, the earth is gaping for us, yet a little while and we shall be carried down into the chambers of death, Lord! Teach us so to number our days that we may apply our hearts unto true, saving wisdom." No doubt, much good may redound to the souls of men this way; and, God be thanked, we can testify that where it has been practiced, people have been made more serious on such sad occasions.

If, therefore, reader, you are one of those that desire to mind your own concern and to stir up others to a timely and thorough preparation for death, we question not but that you will approve of and recommend to others this our proposition, in which again, we assure you (however some censorious persons, that take measures of us by their own narrow spirits, may judge), we do not so much aim at our own private gain as the public of all good Christians.